# The Economic Logic of Late Capitalism and the Inevitable Triumph of Socialism

Simon Glynn

# The Economic Logic of Late Capitalism and the Inevitable Triumph of Socialism

palgrave
macmillan

Simon Glynn
Philosophy
Florida Atlantic University
Boca Raton, FL, USA

ISBN 978-3-030-52666-5 ISBN 978-3-030-52667-2 (eBook)
https://doi.org/10.1007/978-3-030-52667-2



This Palgrave Macmillan imprint is published by the registered company Springer Nature Switzerland AG.
The registered company address is: Gewerbestrasse 11, 6330 Cham, Switzerland

# Preface

Analysis of the Great Recession and the understanding thus derived leads, as the book shows, to the admittedly startling thesis that capitalism has almost run its course, and will inevitably be replaced by socialism.

Thus, while the predatory mortgage lending and overleveraging, which is to say the overextension of credit, was, as has been well established, the immediate cause of the Great Recession, this overextension of credit was a response to a *crisis of overproduction*, which is to say of insufficient economic *demand* for the *supply* of goods and services. A crisis of overproduction, which as Marx argued over a century and a half ago, is rooted in what he identified as a *contradiction at the heart of capitalism*. The contradiction being that the drive for ever increasing efficiency or productivity, that is the precondition of survival in a competitive capitalist economy, puts downward pressure on wages and other benefits, and upward pressure on production, thereby leaving the general population with insufficient money to be able to purchase the goods and services they produce. And although more developed capitalist economies have been able to ameliorate such crises, and the decline and fall of capitalism which Marx argued would inevitably result from this contradiction, by the exploitation of less developed economies, thereby ensuring a cheap *supply* of, therefore affordable, goods and services, and more recently by the aforementioned overextension of credit as a means to buoying up economic *demand* for goods and services, these solutions are, as we shall see, increasingly unsustainable. A circumstance which, portending capitalism's imminent demise, renders a pragmatic and moral comparison of capitalism, as paradigmatically instantiated in the US economy, with socialism, as paradigmatically instantiated in that of China, as timely as it is pressing.

The work is intended to be informative and interesting both to the wide, but by no means necessarily economically specialized, undergraduate, graduate, and professorial academic community, including those in philosophy, political science, political economy, sociology, economic geography and history, and social anthropology, and the like, as well as interdisciplinary studies, and to engage lay readers also. And while in attempting to "bridge" such a wide-ranging readership I shall inevitably be regarded by some as "falling between two (or indeed more) stools," this is, I am afraid, unavoidable given the nature of the project. For instance, issues familiar to the specialist economic audience are not always pursued and analyzed by referencing a large number of confirming, and perhaps dissenting, viewpoints, as they would be in a more specialized, scholarly monograph, while I have sometimes dwelt upon, and even returned at length to, some points which may well go without saying to the economic or political specialist. However, in light of the explication of the currently relatively underrepresented, unusual, and undoubtedly contentious views considered here, I hope that all, including the non-specialist audience who may be encountering some of the idea presented here for the first time, will nevertheless find the arguments and analyses both interesting and informative.

Boca Raton, FL, USA Simon Glynn

# Contents

CHAPTER 1

# Introduction

**Abstract** While the *immediate* cause of the Great Recession of 2008 may have been predatory mortgage and other lax lending and excessive leveraging, which is to say the over extension of credit, this was, in turn, a reaction to free market (*laissez-faire*) *Capitalist* competition. For in putting downward pressure on wages and benefits and upward pressure on production, such competition *inevitably* results in the general public being unable to afford to buy what they produce. A *crisis of overproduction*, which although *temporarily* assuaged by *credit* will, given the downward pressure on wages, inevitably results in default on the concomitant *debt*. The *economic logic of capitalist competition* inevitably results in its ultimate demise therefore inviting both a *pragmatic* and *moral* comparison of (US) capitalism to (Chinese) socialism.

**Keywords** Capitalism • Socialism • Communism • Great Recession • Predatory lending • Leveraging • Crisis of overproduction

## Capitalism and Socialism Defined

Before proceeding to the substantive analysis, I should like, in order to minimize any ambiguity or uncertainly that may otherwise arise, to attempt to define, at an appropriate level of generalization for the task at



S. Glynn, *The Economic Logic of Late Capitalism and the Inevitable Triumph of Socialism*,
https://doi.org/10.1007/978-3-030-52667-2_1

hand, the two most significant concepts, not to say economic systems, being compared and contrasted, here; namely Capitalism and Socialism.

Capitalism then is, in such general terms, an *economic* system in which the *means of production*, (which is to say all capital goods and systems used to produce the goods and services we consume), the *means of distribution* (whether transportation and retail outlets and the like, or electronic networks and grids etc.) and the *means of exchange* (such as currency and banking facilities and the like), together with the naturally occurring *resources* necessary for the production of such goods and services, are overwhelmingly, but not necessarily entirely, owned and directed by private Capitalists or stock holders. A system within which *labor* is usually free to pursue its own interests, but a system which is generally configured so as to predominantly serve the perceived interests of the Capitalists, which is to say to maximize returns on Capital or Profits. And Capitalism is usually, at least in principle, *Competitive*; each private enterprise engaged in so-called *laissez-faire*, or free market, *competition* with other similarly privately owned enterprises, for the same resources, labor, and markets/customers.

Turning now to define Socialism, it is possibly helpful in order to avoid confusions and misconceptions to begin by contrasting it to, and thus distinguishing it from, Communism; an *economic* system in which the *means of production, distribution, and exchange*, not to mention all naturally occurring *resources*, are entirely owned and operated by the government or State. A government or State which directly controls them and their products, including *labor*, ostensibly on behalf and "according to the( ) needs" of the population in general, and the working class or *proletariat* in particular. A proletariat or working class which, although sometimes narrowly misconceived of as only those engaged in physical labor, may be more properly conceived as all those employed in waged labor of any description—be it physical or intellectual (e.g. managerial, administrative, technologically innovative, inspirational, educational, etc.)—and therefore engaged, directly or indirectly, in the gathering of resources, and their transformation into goods and/or the provision of services, and thus in the creation of all real economic value.

Socialism on the other hand, *at least as it is most usually encountered and identified as such in practice*, may be seen as occupying a position between these two (Capitalist and Communist) alternatives. Which is to say, as an *economic* system in which much, although by no means necessarily all, of the *means of production, distribution, and exchange* are publicly owned and operated, and in which the government or State, insofar as it is politically aligned with the socialist economic ethos, regulates the operations of the publically owned and operated sector and determines what it produces, in accordance with the perceived interests and needs of the general public. While the operations of that sector which is either privately owned and operated, or publicly owned and privately operated, is, given the same political alignment, usually subject to extensive regulation in the name of the interests of the general public; although this sector generally remains free to determine what it produces, except in those cases where its *products* are perceived as detrimental to the environment and/or the general public. A system in which the *natural resources* it utilizes may be privately, or publicly, owned, and in which *labor* is free to follow its own interests and to seek employment in any sector, but where the terms and conditions of employment, even in the private sector, are often subject to extensive government regulation, in the perceived interests of the workforce. Yet an *economic* system in which, while profit generating tendencies may be allowed and even encouraged *to some degree* in order to incentivize productivity or efficiency, profits are usually subjected to significant taxation in order to finance projects and so on perceived to be in the public interest. An *economic* system which is therefore, in the final analysis, based upon, and aims to further, *cooperation* between, if not quite all then, the overwhelming majority, to their mutual benefit, even if sometimes at the expense of the profits of a *competitive* capitalist class.

Now it will, of course, be objected, that such neo-Weberian "Ideal Types" are seldom, if indeed ever, encountered in their pure form in the real world. The most obvious exceptions to the nomenclature briefly sketched here being that Capitalism in its actually existing form, is, of course, often subject to some degree of government regulation and taxation in pursuit of socially agreed upon public goals, or conversely, may, largely through its largesse, unduly influence and even capture the political process, and may accordingly be heavily subsidized by general tax revenues, and otherwise assisted by the State, in the interests of private owners or stockholders. And in some cases, it may, so far from being competitive, actually be monopolistic, and in many cases oligopolistic. While on the other hand, the State's control of Communist economic systems may be exercised to the benefit of corrupt political functionaries and administrative bureaucrats rather than in the interests of the working class as a whole and/or the population more generally. A tendency to which Socialism is not entirely immune either. However, as it is not my intention to sharpen such nuanced distinctions, but rather to provide an overarching, and yet hopefully not too superficial, overview of the general tendencies of, and recent development in, contemporary political economy, and as in so doing I will inevitably introduce an analytical framework that will help clarify such distinctions as it contributes to the greater understanding of the very political economies from which it derives—notably the US and China as arguably the two most paradigmatic examples of actually existing Capitalist and Socialist societies, respectively—then it is my hope that the nature of and distinctions between Capitalism and Socialism preliminary sketched here will suffice for now.

* * *

To proceed then, the 2008 economic meltdown in the world's leading capitalist economy, the US, and other capitalist economies, followed by The Great Recession, gave rise to fundamental questions concerning the nature and future viability of capitalism. In response, the capitalist classes and their representatives, ever concerned to protect their privilege, were quick to point to predatory lending—often in the form of so-called subprime mortgages[1]—as the origin of a crisis which they were anxious to insist was largely limited to real estate financing, even as, due to overleveraging,[2] it spilled over into the economy more generally. And

[1] Subprime mortgages are technically loans to individuals with low credit scores, which are often, although not always, *initially* offered at below normal market (or "teaser") interest rates in order to entice those individuals, who might otherwise balk at the cost of the interest payments otherwise entailed by such a mortgage, into taking them on. Individuals who may, if housing values rise, take out second mortgages or home equity loans (collateralized or insured by the increase in value of their housing asset) enabling them to continue paying their mortgages even as interest rates on them are increased to reflect market rates, but who, if property values do not rise (sufficiently) and they are consequently unable to take out such secondary loans, will be particularly vulnerable to such future increases in interest rates and the increased payments they entail.

[2] Lehman Brothers is reported to have had a leveraged debt to asset ratio of 42-fold, or 4200% ["60 Minutes" a CBS television presentation, October 19, 2012]. *Leveraging* being the extension of a loan or credit in excess of the value of the asset or equity *initially* used to back or *collateralize* it. Thus if, for example, a lender lends money to a borrower (e.g. to buy a house), then the borrower's *derivative* promise to pay down the debt (e.g. mortgage) with interest accruing thereto, or *debt obligation,* can then be *securitized,* which is to say sold as a *security* on the financial markets, by the initial lender. This thereby provides that lender with further working capital that can be used to *collateralize* (i.e. underwrite or insure) further loans (e.g. mortgages), and so on and on…so that the lender can make a large number of

although such practices were indeed the immediate cause of the financial crisis, and the eradication of the most obvious rot (e.g. Lehman Brothers and their ilk) and the structural modification of the most obviously over-leveraged assets therefore prevented the immediate collapse of the capitalist system, when analyzed from a wider perspective such predatory lending and overleveraging can be seen and understood to be responses to a *crisis of overproduction* which follows inevitably from the *competitive nature of capitalism*; a competitive capitalist system which therefore seems to be the ultimate cause of a crisis within itself, which will finally lead to its ultimate demise.

That is to say that the struggle for the greatest *efficiency*, which is the inherent precondition of survival in a competitive capitalist system, results in upward pressure on production, and downward pressure on wages, benefits, and other costs of production which largely provide the economic *demand* for the increased production. *A driving up of Supply and a driving down of Demand which, other things being equal, results in falling prices, which clearly threatens the very profitability upon which the survival of capitalism is also dependent. An internal or dialectical contradiction—between efficiency and profitability—at the very heart of capitalism, which* while it *portends its eventually inevitable collapse*, may nevertheless be postponed by demand stimulating credit. A solution which not only ensures continuing, and even increasing, demand for ever more goods and services without requiring profit threatening wage increases or price reductions, but happily, at least for the economic elite, resulted in their accruing yet more profit, in the form of interest on the credit they advanced. Credit which, prior to the 2008 crisis was largely made available through mortgages—collateralized or guaranteed as they were by concrete (or indeed bricks and mortar) assets, which is to say housing—and to a lesser extent through Credit Card, Student Loan and other general household, not to mention national, debt. The profits from the, *wholly unproductive, financial economy* even beginning to rival that from the *real economy productive of*

loans to a far greater value than her/his initial capital. (The ratio of the capital thus acquired to the initial loan, or leverage, being vastly enhanced by subprime loans, having, as they do the potential for increasing interest payments (see footnote 1) to the holder of the debt obligation). While any and all *leveraging* becomes problematic when the value of the asset or assets (e.g. houses), which are ultimately backing or *collateralizing* all such loans, collapses, leaving lenders with little immediate or realistic hope of recouping any large proportion of the value of the debt obligations (e.g. mortgages) upon which further loans (e.g. further mortgages) have been extended or "*leveraged.*"

*the goods and non-financial services*, without which money generated by the financial economy would be entirely worthless. But credit, which having eventually to be repaid, could only ever offer a temporary solution.

Turning then to focus on the housing mortgage market as the main conduit for such credit. In that market *an increase in the availability of mortgages*—financed by the leveraging (or selling on to others) of securitized derivatives (or promises by the borrowers to pay their mortgages)—*drove up the price of housing, thereby increasing the value of the collateral (residences) that underwrote a further increase in mortgages that drove housing prices still higher and so on and on.* This then manifested itself as housing price increase which attracted a secondary, wholly speculative, market that drove up house and other residential prices still further (creating a housing price "bubble") to the point where they were out of the reach of those whose primary *need* was to house themselves and their families; those upon whose demand the price of housing *ultimately* rests. A weakness in demand which eventually resulted in an unloading of speculatively acquired housing, and a surge in the supply thereof, and consequently a *collapse of housing prices*, which is to say of the assets ultimately underwriting the leveraging of securitized mortgage derivatives. This resulted in *a cascading financial crisis, which while indisputably the immediate cause of the Great Recession, was, as the above exposition suggests, ultimately rooted in a crisis of overproduction emanating from the competitive nature of Capitalism.* This then raises the question as to why financial regulators allowed the mortgage crisis to happen? A question which inevitably raises the issue of the relation of the political system of government, and the political class, to the economic (in this case capitalist) class.

Returning then to the economic meltdown and Great Recession as experienced in that most paradigmatically capitalist of economies, the US, and focusing further on the political response thereto, we shall see that this offers as an illuminating demonstration of the nature and priorities of the political class as one could hope for; a political class which did everything in its power to mitigate the impact of such economic setbacks upon the capitalists, even at the expense of the general public. This was achieved, by the government bailouts of the mortgage companies, banks, and other financial institutions which like the tax breaks and even subsidies given to agribusiness, the energy, aviation and a host of other corporations, and the rescue of Chrysler and General Motors, was largely financed and underwritten at the expense of general taxpayers, and by lowering interest rates at the expense of often small (frequently pension) saves. All of which was clearly a radical departure from the *laissez-faire* free market about which the capitalist classes wax so lyrical when subjected to government taxes and regulations. But a departure which in socializing the downside risk even while maintaining the privatization of the upside profits, is a form of government intervention or (corporate) welfare for which the capitalist classes actively lobbied, often through their representatives in government.

Why then, we may ask, did nearly all the politicians, of all political stripes, in fact represent the interests of the capitalist elite and their corporations even at the aforementioned expense of the "people" or public more generally, who in a functioning democracy they would surely represent; why did they orchestrate and implement, rather than opposed, such an inequitable reaction to the economic meltdown? The well-recognized answer being the capture of the political class by the economic elite that is an increasingly prevalent feature of capitalism. A capture, achieved in the US for example as a consequence, in the first instance, of the expense of running for political office, and the corresponding need of candidates to solicit financial contributions, usually from wealthy individual and corporate donors, who consequently constitute or become a *selectorate* who *generally* see to it that only those candidates, of either major political party, who are prepared to represent their interests, are even able to stand for election. A selectorate therefore, who will also see to it that any candidate who is nevertheless able to escape such dependence, and any politician who, for this or any other reason, is willing to stand up to them on behalf of the less affluent, will confront lavishly funded opposition or/and opponents for office. The political power of the capitalist classes being further augmented by their ownership of most of the major mainstream media, and their financing of an extensive network of "think" tanks and lobbyists.

In consequence, the best politicians that money can buy design and oversee the enforcement (or not) of the rules and regulations structuring the market, in such a manner as to ensure that certain individuals or companies (one and the same since Citizens United vs. FEC) benefit. So, far from the *fittest*, in the sense of the most efficiently productive, surviving a supposedly neo-Darwinian struggle for survival, on the contrary it is those whose interests the market is designed to *fit*, who survive and thrive. These are the *crony* capitalists, who thus benefit economically from their financial support of the political class writing the rules in their favor. A circumstance which gives an entirely new meaning to the invisible or hidden hand of the supposedly *laissez-faire* or "free" market, which, so far from being free, is in fact rather expensive. While in addition to the expense of the economic bailouts noted above, *there are*, as we shall see, *any number of* other, often *highly significant, instances of the expense and costs to society at large, of capitalism's pursuit of private profits.*

Nor does the control of the political, and indeed even the judicial, class by the economic elite end there, for when their (the economic elite's) avarice entails their felony violations of both civil and criminal law, including even the most blatantly criminal activity, so far from this resulting in jail time it has typically resulted in non or deferred prosecution agreements, or in fines, representing only the most meager percentage of their ill-gotten gains; fines which, moreover, are levied on corporations rather than individuals.

In sum then, *the capitalists' conforming of the market and market regulations and their enforcement to fit them, obviating their need to prove themselves the fittest in an open and fair competitive struggle for survival, together with the economic bailouts, clearly serve to undermine the two most compelling, if not the only barely credible, arguments for capitalism. (1) That free market competition, supposedly characteristic of capitalism, ensures that only the fittest (in the limited sense of the most efficient) will survive and prosper, thereby promoting the optimal deployment of resources and (2) That in the event of failure it is the capitalist, rather than society at large, who will bear the cost; and that consequently, the capital investment necessary for production will only be forthcoming if the risk individuals or institutions bear by investing is compensated for by profit from those investments that are successful!*

Furthermore, an arguably even more significant, adverse consequence of the capture of the political class by the economic elite is that it has resulted in the ascendency of Monetarist or *Supply Side* economics. For although the bailouts resulted in making the financial institutions solvent, not only did it largely neglect "Keynesian" *Demand Side stimulus*, which, had a significant proportion of the bailout financing been provided to the large number of households that were underwater (owing more on their mortgages than the declining value of their residencies) in their mortgages, would have thereby restored their solvency and purchasing power or demand, but it saved the financial institutions, as just explicated, at the *expense* of the public in general, thereby actively *suppressing their demand, and thus exacerbating rather than ameliorating the ongoing crisis of overproduction.*

Indeed, although flush with bailout cash the financial institutions were therefore in a position to extend credit to the general public, whether mortgage borrowers or not, and in doing so to thereby stimulate demand in the *real or productive economy*, in light of the immediately prevailing depression in the regular economy resulting from reduced demand due to increasing mortgage, general household, and other, debt, these institutions saw that it would be much more profitable *for them*, in the short run at least, if, instead, they invested in themselves, which is to say in the *financial economy*. This then resulted in a slow or lackluster recovery in the real economy, even as, by buying back their own shares, they inflated the values of the stock and stock options held by senior executives, and generated enormous profits for other shareholders, thereby also reaping large performance linked bonuses for themselves; and, in a spate of acquisitions and mergers of financial institutions made these institutions, already bailed out at taxpayer expense because they were apparently "too big (and interconnected) to fail" without jeopardizing the entire capitalist edifice, even bigger and more interconnected!

Moreover, returning to the aforementioned dialectical contradiction at the heart of capitalism which initiated the crisis, while in previous epochs *colonial*, and later *economic neo-colonial exploitation* of the labor and resources of the less technologically developed economies, by and to the advantage of the more technologically developed economies, initially forestalled any crisis of overproduction,[3] the "tide is turning" in that such international commerce has, for reasons to be explored in detail, increasingly taken the form of ever more competition emanating from the previously colonized or/and less developed economies that are a part of the increasingly globalized free market. Growing competition which, demanding ever greater efficiency, has driven the wages and benefits etc. of those in the developed economies, and consequently the demand emanating therefrom, down. Thus, although the international extension of capitalism

[3] Colonialism simply requisitioned the resources and labor of the colonized nations, while neo-colonialism props up, or even installs, elites prepared to collude in the extraction of resources and the supply of cheap labor to their patrons. In either case the exploitation of such cheap labor and resources thus derived from the less developed economies enables the more advanced economies to keep production costs down even while paying their own, domestic or national, workforce, sufficiently well to enable them to afford the finished goods and services to whose production they make some contribution. A circumstance which ensures the continuing profitability of the advanced economies, until such arrangements change.

has certainly lifted some in the developing economies out of poverty, so far from being, as is often claimed, "a rising tide that lifts *all* boats," the "turning tide" has meant that it is increasingly doing so at the expense of many of those in the advanced economies. Indeed, it has often resulted, and is continuing to result, in those economies, whether developed or developing, which are "unseaworthy," which is to say insufficiently or poorly resourced and/or skilled and/or administered, becoming "underwater" wrecks. While furthermore, although the admitted increase in the wages of some in the ***developing*** "second world" economies, and profits from resource extraction from ***undeveloped*** "third world" counties, may give rise to new international markets, so far from their being sufficient to compensate for the loss of demand from workers in the developed economies, if and insofar as the international or globalized market continues to be dominated by the same competitive ethos and consequent economic logic as are the capitalist economies prevalent in it, then, as we shall explore in more detail, the new economic world order will be no less a victim of the crisis of overproduction stemming therefrom than are individual capitalist economies. This then making any increases in the standard of living of the second and third world economies unsustainable or temporary. *The economic logic of the struggle for efficiency*—defined as the ratio of the value of output to the cost of input, or productivity—*on which capitalism prides itself, inevitably leading to a "race to the bottom" between nations, as it does between workers, as each competes with the others to supply labor, and in the case of nations, resource also, at a cheaper price than their rivals.*

Furthermore, while the spread of capitalism may have enabled, and in some cases may be continuing to allow, some, previously ***underdeveloped*** capitalist economies, and even their workers also, to prosper, not only have they often done so, as just outlined, at the expense of the developed economies, but, as we shall see they have also done so by drawing in and exploiting those even further down, what thus becomes, the ever expanding base of a pyramid of production. A pyramid of production which, as such, resembles nothing so much as a gigantic *Ponzi Scheme (as exemplified in chain letters). A pyramid which will, like the Ponzi Scheme, inevitably collapse as the system runs out of suckers—in this case exploitable labor and cheap resource providers—to draw into its base.*

Finding fewer and fewer uncontested opportunities to draw other nations into the base of the pyramid then, and facing increasing global competition, particularly from (as we shall argue) essentially Socialist China, the Capitalist US economy has been forced to imposed tariffs, ostensibly on the grounds that, due to the Chinese government's intervention in *their* (the Chinese) economy such action is necessary in order to "level the playing field." A "justification" which, in view of the well-worn capitalist adage that government is incapable of running anything anywhere nearly as efficiently as supposedly free market capitalist economies, would appear to be as heterodox as the US government's intervention in their own national economy, which is, as we shall see, as massive as it is extensive!

Indeed, unlike the Chinese government's involvement in their economy, which, guided—at least internally and when not interacting with *competitive capitalist* economies—by a socialist *cooperative* ethos or ideology as it is, lifted an enormous number and percentage of the Chinese population out of poverty, the US government's intervention in their national economy, *increasingly aimed, as we shall see, at ensuring and boosting capitalism's profitability*, has not only been accompanied by falling median wages in the US, but has resulted in ballooning annual deficits and massive unfunded mandates (Future Social Security and other pensions and Medicare costs, etc.). This then in contrast to earlier US government intervention, which, in contrast, generally aimed—prior to neo-liberal rollback from the Regan era on—*at funding socially useful Research and Development (R&D)* which resulted, along with other factors to be analyzed in some detail, in an unprecedented boom in the economy that made Lyndon Johnson's Great Society, or social welfare programs, possible. Investment in R&D, which—by enabling the production of goods and services either more *efficiently*, or of a *sort or type* and/or *quality* that others are unable to match, and thereby enabling wage rises that do not threaten profitability—were it to be combined with infrastructure investment would, along with adequately funded, demand stimulating, welfare programs, certainly help, in the short term at least, to ameliorate recurrent crises of overproduction.

However, globalization, and the free flow of technological information and intellectual (e.g. research as well as administrative, management etc.) labor which it has facilitated, while boosting *production*, has rendered the aforementioned advantages that the developed nations are able to derive from extensive investment in R&D increasingly difficult to maintain or sustain. Consequently, *so far from economic competition stimulating innovation it has, as the flow of information and expertise becomes ever more "frictionless," resulted—at least in a global economy dominated by the capitalist imperative of economic profitability—in a free rider reticence to invest in R&D*, which is to say in an attempt to reap the benefits, without incurring the costs, of others' investment. While as with technological investment, so too with investment in "education" or job training. The "brain drain" to the developed and rapidly developing economies in addition making it more difficult for the others to competitively move up the pyramid of production, and avail themselves of the benefit of the "rising tide" of global economic activity. All of which stands in contrast to socialist economies which, ideologically committed to *cooperation* to the mutual benefit of all, would be even more prepared than they currently are to invest in R&D and education to the mutual benefit of all, were it not for the fact that in order to survive in and derive any benefits from a global economy currently dominated by the competitive capitalist ethos, they must adopt at least some of its competitive characteristics. While it was most surely the recognition of the greater efficacy of *cooperation* as compared with *competition*, that, despite the rhetorical claim that *competition* inevitably spurs innovative advancement, "when the chips were down" the US funded Manhattan Project for example, was a government directed, cooperative, and thus synergy producing, endeavor. The advantage of adopting government directed and funded, and thus communist or socialist style, economic systems—which additionally may, generally, benefit from the fact that government-run industries, unburdened with profit taking, are able to funnel a much higher percentage of their profits back into growth stimulating economic reinvestment—being, as we shall see, clearly evident in the much more rapid overall development of such economies than those of the capitalist West.

Furthermore, unhindered post the 2008 economic meltdown by the need to bail out capitalist financial and other institutions, the Chinese have instead invested heavily in R&D in advances transportation, aircraft, communication, solar, electric, robotic, production, autonomous vehicle, semi-conductor, quantum computing, artificial intelligence, pharmaceutical and the other technologies constitutive of their "China 2025" advanced technology project, all of which stimulate current domestic demand driven expansion. While, to revert to the earlier point, instead of taking a large percentage of the wealth generated as profits, much of it has been reinvested in its "Belt and Road" international infrastructure and resource development scheme. An undertaking which, in contrast to capitalism's zero-sum[4] economic neo-colonial attempt to extract as much private profit as possible, at the expense of those neo-colonized, has predominantly taken the form of mutually beneficial, win/win, cooperative engagement and partnership. Thus, with such technological advances, access to resources, transportation infrastructure, and much international good will, China has positioned itself for ever more rapid future economic expansion!

In contrast, capitalist governments, wary of any such cooperative ideology that would threaten competitively derived private wealth, have been hostile to any recognition of and accommodation to any such cooperative ideology, often to the considerable detriment of their nations' national and international interests. Consequently, they have pursued international trade agreement and practices, which, *in the interests of protecting profits*, establish patent and copyright restrictions, technological transfer limits and other intellectual property rights that *inhibit the free flow of technology and ideas that would be of such global benefit to all of humanity*. And upon being forced to acknowledge that this entails the inhibition of the free market that they affect to promote, they fall back on ostensibly "strategic interest," "national security," and, most absurdly, "ecological," justifications for doing so. And yet they bat not an eye at the environmental and health costs of anthropogenic global climate change, and its associated sea level rise, increased hurricane activity, flooding and drought, resulting from the activity of their fossil fuel industries, and generally show as little concern for environmental refugees—who unable to sustain agricultural production in face of such climate change, are forced off their land—as they do for the refugees resulting from the politically destabilizing collusion with foreign elites often necessary to secure carbon emitting oil and other resources, and to otherwise further their own, private, economic ends.

Indeed, even the aforementioned internal economic contradiction within capitalism notwithstanding, many of these other problems seem, in and of themselves, sufficient to suggest that it is no less *pragmatically* than *morally desirable* to abandon it.[5] Thus, in general, just as unrestrained competition for diminishing stocks of fish would result in dire consequences

[4] A zero-sum game or situation is where the gains of one individual, group or class are derived at the equal expense of another, there therefore being no net gains or losses.

[5] Socialism, as ideologically *cooperatively* aimed at the good of all, is, if not entirely identical with Utilitarian morality's promotion of "the sum total of human happiness," very close to it.

for all, while cooperative agreement to limit catches enables the shoals to recover to the advantage of all, similarly not only does economic *competition* inevitably result in a *lose/lose* crisis of overproduction, but in conflict, including wars, in the competition for resources, and even, counterintuitively, as outlined, in the limiting of technological potential, not to mention human potential limiting poverty. While in contrast *cooperation* not only enables all to be paid sufficiently to be collectively able to afford what is produced, thus avoiding a crisis of overproduction as well as mitigating against the limiting of technological potential and human potential limiting poverty, but also avoids wars over, often diminishing, natural resources! A *win/win* outcome that promotes socio-political harmony. Moreover, in addition to being environmentally responsible, to the benefit of all, socially concerned and accountable production would seek to reduce the production of goods of little social utility, and also try to ensure, so far as possible, that jobs were, if not enhancing, certainly not, or at least less, stultifying, even at the cost of limiting productivity; those stultifying jobs that were ineliminable being sufficiently highly paid to enable short working hours. All of which would, in turn, lead to less *extreme and often conspicuous consumption* by which many attempt to compensate for unsatisfying jobs, and those whose education, instead of facilitating self-actualization, has been largely restricted to job training, often turn in their attempts to alleviate boredom and/or to garner the attention, affection and esteem, that a genuinely self-actualizing education might both have to some degree afforded even while, in any event, rendering such appreciation less important. All of which would undoubtedly alleviate pressures on the natural environment, and therefore further reduce many of the tensions productive of global conflict.

And to the objection that all of this entails government intervention, and that although such socialist intervention may be fine in theory, it is unworkable in practice, we will recall that, as we have seen, government intervention by the Chinese is generally regarded as accounting in large part for their economic growth, and that the US government's intervention in the US economy is not only, as we shall see in detail, extensive, but widely regarded by its capitalist patrons, as highly beneficial. The only major difference between the two being that intervention in a capitalist economy/society is predominantly aimed at promoting the power and *freedom* of the already well of *To* profit and so on, even at the expense of the less well of, and poor, while socialist intervention understood in the conventional sense is, of course, preponderantly aimed at promoting the wellbeing of all, and their *freedom From* poverty and its consequences.

For instance, Chinese government measures such as the extension of rural pensions, access to health care regardless of capacity to pay, minimum living allowances, and the National Development and Reform Commission, which keeps a check on price collusion and cheating with regard to basic foodstuffs and other commodities, have provided a substantial social safety net, as empirically evidenced by the aforementioned near eradication of poverty in China. A practicality that stands in marked contrast to capitalism, as is demonstrated by the fact that, in an overwhelmingly capitalist world, which, it is estimated, could produce enough food to feed everyone on the planet at least 8 times over, around 15 Million people a year (which is to say about one every 2 seconds) die from malnutrition and malnutrition-related diseases, largely because it is not *profitable* to do so!

And to the objection that, so far from being Socialist, the Chinese Economy is Capitalist, it is observed that although parts of the Chinese economy, and in particular those trading and otherwise interacting with capitalist economies, have indeed, as noted, been forced to take on certain competitive characteristics, and that in order to facilitate the profit generation which *in some circumstances* encourage productivity and efficiency, some parts of the Chinese economy are indeed either (i) Privately Owned and Operated or (ii) Publically Owned and Privately Operated, nevertheless, as *per* socialism, these sectors are subject to extensive government regulation and taxation in the public interest. While in addition the Chinese government also maintains extensive indirect control over the private sector, via a comprehensively regulated Financial System, the lending priorities of which therefore directly reflect socialist policies. Furthermore, much of the Chinese economy, particularly those parts producing more fundamental, if not essential, products are often (iii) Collectively, or/and Town or City, Owned and Operated enterprises. While most significantly (iv) the Chinese government or State Owns and Operates core Energy and Power Generation and Distribution, Iron and Steel Production, key Transportation and Vehicle Production, Space Exploration, Telecommunications, major Media Production and Broadcasting Outlets, and Education, as well as Armaments.

In sum then the choice appears obvious to all but those who benefit, albeit, for reasons we have seen, inevitably temporarily, from exploitation of others and the environment. On the one hand short-term *zero-sum*, and long-term *lose/lose capitalist competition* which, as a precondition of survival requires maximum efficiency, not only at the expense of environmental, social and human welfare, but which, in driving down wages as it drives up production, thereby inevitably precipitates crises of overproduction; ameliorable in the short term by the overextension of private credit, and in the longer term by taxpayer funded, government bailouts. A perverted or negative socialism, which takes from the poor to give to the rich, and which, if consumer/taxpayer demand is nevertheless to be maintained as it must be to escape the crisis, ultimately entails an increasing unsustainable national debt, which will therefore inevitably lead to total economic collapse, and the civil unrest, or worse, accompanying it. On the other hand, by way of contrast *win/win socialist cooperation*, which in attempting to ensure that the economy serves the general public, rather than the other way around, and concomitantly prioritizing human economic, social, psychological, and environmental welfare over profits—in line with the principle of diminishing marginal utility[6]—spreads the economic and other benefits deriving from the economy widely. *A strategy, which, in maintaining robust demand, avoids the economic and environmental, not to mention social and human, catastrophe, portended by capitalist competition, not despite, but indeed because, of its promoting human, and indeed social, wellbeing.*

[6]As this principle notes, there comes a point where the *increase* in wellbeing or *utility* an individual or group derive for every additional unit of inputs of a resource, or the money they are able to command—their "bang for the buck"—begins to *diminish*. Thus, for example, the increase in wellbeing or utility that an otherwise starving individual might expect to derive from, say, an extra $5 a day, is, other things being equal, generally much greater than that which a Millionaire might expect to derive from the same $5. A fact which therefore tends, at least on Utilitarian moral (which, as we shall see, is to say broadly humanitarian) grounds, to encourage spreading the benefits derived from an economy more widely and equally than, typically, does capitalist competition.

CHAPTER 2

# The Great Recession, Its Immediate Cause and Government Intervention: The Purportedly Free Market Designed by the "Invisible" or "Hidden Hand" of the Economic Elite, Conformity to the Market Therefore as Conformity to Their Interests, and the Survival of the "Fittest" Being the Survival of Those Who Can Have the Market Best Fit Them

**Abstract** Quantitative Easing and Troubled Asset Relief, which were government responses to the Great Recession, are revealed as species of *corporate welfare* which abandon free market capitalism for an *inverted socialism*, which takes from the less well-off to give to the economic elite and their financial institutions. Moreover the "free" market is economically shaped and politically sanctioned to fit the interests of this elite. Consequently, so far from fostering the optimal deployment of resources, the "survival of the fittest" is the survival of those who can have the market regulations most closely *fit* their interests. While the injunction that the political, social, cultural, and individual conform to the dictates of the market is therefore the injunction that they serve the interests of the economic elite.



S. Glynn, *The Economic Logic of Late Capitalism and the Inevitable Triumph of Socialism*,
https://doi.org/10.1007/978-3-030-52667-2_2

**Keywords** Free market • Corporate welfare • Inverted socialism • Survival of the "Fittest"

Following the 2008 collapse of world financial markets, capitalism appeared to some to be on its deathbed. Yet although it was on life support for a while, nevertheless the prophets of profits insisted that reports of its demise were greatly exaggerated. Thus indeed, in the world's leading, not to say paradigmatically, capitalist economy, which is to say the US, once the so-called toxic assets, composed largely of unsound or/and over-leveraged[1] securities owned by banks and other financial institutions had been purged via the Troubled Asset Relief Program (TARP), and the resulting void filled with massive (initially $85 Billion per month!) infusions of equity or working capital via "Quantitative Easing" (QE) (by which the Federal Reserve created the "money" or liquid capital it used to buy financial "assets" from banks and other financial institutions) it was insisted that the patient's condition had stabilized. Not that the road to full recovery would be undemanding or short. Although at least insofar as, painful as it may have been, the tourniquet of austerity, designed to staunch the potentially inflationary hemorrhaging of monies to welfare, social, and other government-financed programs, was applied and/or further tightened, and so long as regulators ensured that the patient curtail previously irresponsibly speculative lending behavior, capitalism, it was argued, would be eventually returned to the rudest of rude good health.

Why? Because other things being equal, the increase in the supply of money to the financial institutions resulting from these actions meant more money being available, and consequently lower interest rates, both for responsible investment (thus stimulating the *supply* of goods and services) and for responsible consumer credit (thus stimulating consumer *demand* for goods and services); money which, whether as a result of the former, as *Monetarist or supply side economists* insist, or the latter, as the *"Keynesian" or demand side economists* will argue, or both, would in any event stimulate the economy, and thereby save capitalism.

One point worth noting, however, is that in light of such government-financed corporate welfare, not to mention the subsequent ostensible

[1] See Chapter 1, footnote 2.

regulatory restriction of irresponsibly excessive risk taking that supposedly accompanied it, as well as more direct government bailouts of major financial and other corporations, the capitalism that emerged from this process was certainly not of the free market *laissez-faire* variety about which economic neo-liberals wax so lyrical. Not that such an edifice ever truly existed anyhow. For, so far from being an inevitable outgrowth, or at least a positive reflection, of the natural order, the much vaunted putatively "free" market is, of course, culturally or socially constituted from the ground up; originally on the basis of taboo, custom, and tradition, and, more recently, upon the explicit laws and regulation characteristic of what Max Weber dubbed "legal rational" societies. Rules, regulations, and laws which, in addition to defining the market, even if not always vigilantly observed, much less enforced (e.g., by the Securities and Exchange Commission), nevertheless restrict its supposed freedom to a considerable extent.

In view of this it should be clear that, notwithstanding shrill insistence to the contrary, so far from the "fittest" who survive the supposed Darwinian struggle for supremacy being the most powerful or efficient, rather they are those who so configure themselves as to "fit" most closely within the framework of such regulations, rules, laws, and so on. Or, alternatively, they are those who are most able—through the strategic deployment of wealth to finance politician's campaigns and the ability to offer future employment to compliant government regulators (the revolving door) and the like—to ensure that the regulatory framework is configured and enforced, (or not), so as to "fit" (rather than inhibit) them and their economic interests and activities![2] Because, of course, politicians of all major political parties, and by extension their administrative appointees, know exactly who they really work for or represent; and for the most part, and certainly in the US, they clearly work, at least in the first instance, not for the *electorate* but for the *selectorate*; which is to say those wealthy donors who, by underwriting the enormous cost of running for office, delineate a closely circumscribed range of just those candidates who will promote, or at least not seriously challenge, their financial interests,

[2] Thus, as explicated here the term "*fittest*" has at least two distinct, although admittedly related, meanings; the first being directly related to pure strength or power, understood as the property of, for example, a robust individual or corporation, irrespective of the environment, and the second having the connotation of that which fits into its environment, or has its environment so configured as to fit it, in the best possible way, thus making it at *ease* with it, rather than *dis-eased* and thus under threat of extinction.

thereby promoting the election and re-election of the compliant.[3] While those who oppose the interests of corporations, and of the wealthy elite, find themselves facing lavishly funded opponents, who are thus in a position to run extensive negative campaign advertisements. Opponents who, released in the US from transparent disclosure of their *donors* by the Supreme Court's *Citizens Unite* decision, can therefore all the more uninhibitedly serve their "*owners*'" interests without fear of public scrutiny revealing who they really work for!

All of which then gives a wholly new, and more salient, meaning to the "invisible" or "hidden" hand of which "free market" economists have, at least since the time of Adam Smith, been so enamored. A hand which, far from being, as *laissez-faire* neo-liberals would have us believe, the *anonymous* hand of supposedly *natural* market forces, is revealed as the hidden hand of the corporations and the economic elite who, through their political cohorts, largely determine and enforce (or not), the laws, rules, and regulations which delineate or define the market, and thereby help ensure their success.[4]

In light of this then, the insistence by economic neo-liberals that, instead of governments seeking to regulate the "free" market in pursuit of the interests of the general public, they should, along with those they represent, accommodate themselves to market forces, so far from being an injunction to conform to some sort of natural order, is clearly revealed as nothing less than an insistence that *political* institutions, not to mention *individuals*' psychological values, attitudes, and aspirations, physical and intellectual skills, capacities, and development, cultural relations and social activities, and so on should be subjugated to the *financial* interests of the

[3] Although money alone is not *sufficient* to ensure election and/or re-election, given the cost of making and running campaign advertisements, organizing, staffing, and financing field offices, canvassing, and turning out the vote, it is clearly *necessary*. Thus, the total cost of the US federal elections of 2016 for example, in which less than a handful of seats in either the House or the Senate were won by challengers to incumbents, or otherwise changed hands, was estimated to be over $6.4 Billion, while if other, State and Municipal, elections are also added in, total estimates are of the order of $10 Billion!

[4] During the tenure of the *Democratic* Obama administration, following the passage of the Dodd-Frank Act—which was to a large extent programmatic, leaving much of the detail to be hammered out subsequently—market regulators met with Wall Street executives, whose activities the bill was aimed at regulating, over 2000 times, but met with pro-reform groups much less than a tenth as often. And under the Trump administration an initially Republican-controlled Congress was put to work attempting to gut even the comparatively weak regulations that resulted from these, heavily finance industry influenced, negotiations.

*economic* oligarchs[5] and their financial institutions, who are the hidden hands behind the laws, rules, and regulations structuring these markets![6]

[5] I use the term economic oligarch here and elsewhere, as well as the term financial oligarch, to designate a wealth economic elite and its members who are able, through their and/or their institutions' wealth, to exert much influence on political decision-making, especially in so far as it effects the economic system and their capacity to accrue further wealth.

[6] For instance, would-be workers submit to, and themselves pay for, "education" or job training regimes which shape them and their concerns, and configure their characteristics and skills, as precisely as possible to those demanded by the market. Which, insofar as the political system which delineates the market is enthrall to the wealthy elite, is to say as closely as possible to those characteristics and skills which wealthy investors can most profit from!

CHAPTER 3

# Inverted Socialism: Robbing from the Poor to Give to the Rich, by the Best Politicians Money Can Buy

**Abstract** The economic elite, confident in light of their 2008 economic collapse and subsequent bailout that the political class will underwrite their reckless and exploitative financial behavior, vehemently oppose regulatory reform. While in light of lackluster demand from the general public, left all the more impecunious from largely financing this bailout, financial institutions did not invest the bailout money in the *real* economy, but mainly in the *financial* economy (themselves). Lucrative in that the government taxes on the general public that helped finance the bailout thereby contributed both the general public's need for the money and the financial institutions money to satisfy that need, as they then lent the general public back what was/had been their own money at vastly inflated rates. Moreover, largely eschewing the bailing out of underwater mortgage borrowers, economic elites further profited enormously from buying up foreclosed housing at rock bottom prices!

**Keywords** Bailout • Shell game • Dodd-Frank • Asset bubbles • Debt/asset ratio, Inequality

Notwithstanding their supposed commitment to the ostensibly "free market" designed to their advantage, the allegedly neo-liberal economic oligarchs had absolutely no objection to government intervention in this market, in the form of a bailout of the major financial institutions and

 
S. Glynn, *The Economic Logic of Late Capitalism and the Inevitable Triumph of Socialism*,
https://doi.org/10.1007/978-3-030-52667-2_3

other corporations, in which they were major stakeholders; at least until after the event! On the contrary, *their* political representatives, and these representatives' administrative appointees actively lobbied for and counseled it. While in light of the cost of such bailouts—both in terms of taxes, and, in the case of QE, the downward pressure on interest accruing to thrifty savers, and upward or inflationary pressure on the price of goods and services resulting from this increase in the supply of money—it should be clear that, so far from being free, the market they championed is, on the contrary, rather expensive!

On the other hand, having been the *beneficiaries* of government intervention in the form of bailouts from a financial meltdown which resulted in the loss of more than 8 Million jobs in the US and the wiping out of almost $13 Trillion of household wealth, along with a precipitous drop in housing prices which left approximately 17 Million US households "underwater"[1] with their mortgages, the economic elite and their corporations have, through their political representatives and *their* administrative appointees, lobbyists and lawyers, and so on, done, and continue to do, everything they can to oppose much of the government intervention in the form of regulatory reforms (such as those initially proposed by the Dodd-Frank Act) aimed at reducing the risk of future meltdowns.[2] For by (i) Ensuring that borrowers or consumers get clear and accurate information regarding the previously hidden fees, abusive terms, and deceptive practices so long a major source of revenue for financial institutions purveying mortgages, home equity loans, credit cards, student loans, and other forms of credit financing; and (ii) Attempting to close loopholes that allow hedge funds, mortgage brokers, over-the-counter derivatives and asset-backed securities to go largely unregulated; as well as (iii) Imposing capital requirements aimed at limiting the over leveraging[3] of assets, Dodd-Frank, as the elite correctly insist, sought to place limits on

[1] "Underwater" is the popular term used to describe a situation in which—as in the meltdown under discussion where increasing numbers of the homes of defaulting mortgage borrowers came onto the market just as, due to the tightening of credit and concomitant difficulty of obtaining new mortgages, demand for residencies fell—the price of homes falls so much that even those who may have paid down their mortgages to a considerable extent, find that their outstanding mortgage debt is greater than the market value of their home.

[2] See Chapter 2, footnote 4, while in addition Trump appointed avowed opponent of the Consumer Financial Protection Bureau, Mick Mulvaney as its director, who subsequently fired all 25 members of its advisory board.

[3] See Chapter 1, footnote 2.

individual liberty or freedom; notably their (the elite's) liberty and freedom to exploit their privilege, and the general public, to the hilt!

And yet as the shrewd observer will surely see, by curtailing predatory lending practices and the overleveraging of financial institutions' assets and so on, such regulations would protect not only borrowers or consumers, but lenders, or the economic elite and their corporate financial institutions, also. Borrowers by ensuring that they do not incur debt obligations that they cannot meet, which therefore also protects lenders in that they are not left holding unpayable, and thus worthless, debt obligations. And lenders more directly by ensuring that they themselves, do not, by irresponsible lending on unsound or/and overleveraged assets, hold massive amounts of inadequately collateralized debt obligation, the default on even a small percentage of which might force them into bankruptcy. For while maximum leveraging of debt to asset ratios—which is to say the proportion of the credit a lender can extend to borrowers relative to the lender's assets—undoubtedly maximizes the *potential* returns (in the form of the total interest payable by borrowers on such maximized or extensive debt) on the lender's initial assets, *other things being equal* it clearly does so at the cost of increasing the risk of default, and thus the *probability*, of substantial long-term cost to,[4] and ultimately bankruptcy of, the lender. Consequently, to the degree that the allure of maximizing *potential* returns is unconstrained, the results will range from instability and the familiar ("Malthusian") cyclical oscillations of the economy as asset bubbles, fueled by easy credit, periodically burst and are subsequently re-inflated, to the catastrophic self-destruction of financial institutions, together with the collapse of the increasingly dense and complexly interconnected system of financial markets by or through which such institutions are related to each other.

Therefore even though the reining in of high risk and inadequately collateralized loans or/and overleveraged assets undoubtedly puts downward pressure on *short-term returns*, given that it clearly helps ensure the *long-term stability* of financial markets, and survival of financial institutions, it would, *on the face of it*, seem strange, given their stake in such financial institutions and financial markets, that the economic elite, so far from embracing such regulation, through their lobbyists and finance industry

[4] Individual instances of default *risk*, when aggregated with sufficient numbers of other such instances, or taken over a long enough time, will inevitably manifest themselves as *costs*.

and political cohorts, did, and continue to do, everything possible to curb it. Haven't they learned anything from the recent crisis, we may ask?

Of course they have. What they learned, as early as the late 1980s, from the government bailout of the Savings and Loans, and the Federal Reserve (Fed) supervised $3.6 Billion bailout of Long-Term Capital Management in the late 1990s, as well as from the 2008 crisis, is that in the event of a market meltdown the best politicians money can buy[5] will do everything they can to ensure that it will not be the economic elite who will bear the cost of clearing up inadequately collateralized loans and their derivatives (the so-called toxic assets). But rather, as the $180 Billion bailout of American International Group (AIG),[6] and myriad other financial institutions confirmed, it will ultimately be the general public who will foot the bill. And they will do so either directly, by the taxes required to finance the buying up of overleveraged and otherwise troubled "Assets" and/or to service the financial deficits resulting therefrom, or more circuitously through QE, which by increasing the supply of money results both in more money chasing borrowers, thus *driving down returns* on interest rate linked "cash" savings of small savers and their pensions, and more money initially chasing the same number of goods and services, thus *driving up prices.* A circumstance which clearly squeezes the thrifty members of the middle classes from both ends.

Clearly then, not only, as previously noted, do we not have anything like a free market, but, as we can now see, we don't even have capitalism, but rather we have socialism, albeit of *a particularly perverse, kind.* A kind *of socialism by which working and middle-class employees—upon whose (physical and intellectual) labor and consumer spending, corporate profits and returns on investment are ultimately dependent—who pay income taxes at the standard rate (and thereby already finance much of the cost of welfare and defense, as well as public "education"/job training and economic infrastructure, from which capitalism benefits) bail out those members of the economic elite such as bankers, hedge fund managers, and large corporations, as well as the already wealthy who invest with and in such financial institutions*

[5] See Chapter 2, footnote 3.

[6] American International Group, most significantly, insured financial institutions against bad debt (by offering credit default swaps on collateralized debt obligations) thus enabling many such institutions, that might otherwise have balked at the substantial "downside" risk that was a concomitant of trading in such potentially highly profitable securitized derivatives, to insure against, or "lay off," this risk.

*and corporation; an economic elite who are typically taxed at a considerably lower rate than their middle-class saviors!*

Thus, hedge fund managers and their ilk—the 7 highest paid of whom "earned" more than $1 Billion a year *each* for *every* in the ten years prior to the onset of the Great Recession, and the top 25 of whom currently make (or at least prior to the coronavirus pandemic, made) an average of over $850 Million a year—have worked out, or perhaps we had better say, have (by way of contributions to politicians' campaign costs) *bought* themselves, a sweetheart deal, by which their earnings are declared as "carried interest" and thereby taxed at a considerably lower rate than the middle classes. A situation which, despite assurances to the contrary made by the Trump junta, was, of course, unchanged by the 2018 Tax "Reform" Bill. Indeed, even those multi-Billionaire capitalists who are not Hedge Fund managers are taxed at rates well below those levied on the middle classes. Thus, Billionaire investor Warren Buffett's marginal tax rate of around 17% is, as to his credit he has repeatedly pointed out, much lower than that of his secretary, and multi-Millionaire Mitt Romney routinely pays less than 14% of his income as taxes, although the marginal rate for most members of the middle class is about double that. While a vast proportion of other "high net worth" individuals benefit from structured investments, accounts, and trusts, often set up in offshore tax-havens, specifically for tax avoidance, and, as both the Panama and the Paradise Papers show, often illegal, tax evasion, purposes.

And turning from individuals to corporations, although the Top Corporate Rate was *nominally* 35%, according to the Government Accountability Office (GAO) US corporations paid an average *effective* Tax Rate of around 14% on what they declare; while in 2012 for example, not untypically, *over 42% of U.S. Corporations with at least $10 Million in assets paid no income tax at all.* Furthermore it is estimated that US corporations currently hold in excess of $2.5 Trillion of untaxed money overseas. However, not content with merely maintaining the *status quo* the 2018 Tax Reform Bill cut the *Nominal* Corporate tax rate by over a third, to 21%, and gave over $40 Billion in additional tax breaks in 2018 and over $60 Billion by 2024, to "pass through" companies, thus increasing whatever may in any case be adding to the National Debt by a *further* $1.9 Trillion over the next ten years according to the non-partisan Congressional Budget Office. A debt which will, if the financial oligarchs continue to get their way, then be used to justify further cuts on top of the ones already taking effect in food stamps and other nutritional programs, Medicare and

Medicaid, special education and rehabilitation services, direct student loans and college student aid, and so on.

Moreover, as if such an inequitable differentiation in tax rates did not sufficiently worsen the already glaring economic inequality in the US, the reduction in government-funded programs and services, and the cutbacks in corporate assistance for employee healthcare and pensions, not to mention the precipitous fall in home equity (to which we shall return at length presently) all resulting from the economic meltdown, further exacerbated it. *Thus, the middle classes were, and are increasingly, forced to turned to the banks and other financial institutions—who, in the name of QE, the government had given or lent money to at no or very low interest rates (not exceeding 0.5%)—to borrow (back) money (on credit cards, etc., typically at interest rates of between 11% and 29%), in order to cover the personal deficit resulting from their comparatively high taxes which provided the money (or the collateral which ensured confidence in fiat money) that the government had given or lent to these financial institutions in the first place! A "Shell Game,"*[7] *which although illegal in most places, is seen in the US as a central component, if not the very beating heart, of finance capitalism!*

Now given the obvious, and stunning, inequity of the nature, terms and conditions of the bailout, how, we may ask, did the economic elite's political representatives and *their* appointees manage to persuade opinion leaders and the general public (whose interests they ostensibly represent) and those few progressive politicians who—by virtue of their genuine popularity with their constituents, had managed to avoid over dependence on corporate, or corporation promoting, campaign finance contributions and the like in order to gain or stay in office—genuinely attempt to align themselves with the public interest, of the need for such action? The answer seems to be that they were able to persuade even them that the cost of inaction would be even greater.

[7] Thus like the typical "shell game" in which a small object, such as a pea, is placed under one of three shells, which are then moved around so rapidly that the "punter" or "mark" losses track of which shell the pea is under, here *the taxpayer's money, first taken by the government, is then either handed off to* (or backs the creation of fiat money handed off to) *the financial institutions* (at low interest rates), *with the consequence that the confused taxpayer or "mark" often rendered relatively impecunious due to such taxation, has to turn to these financial institutions to borrow (back)* (at high interest rates) *the money she/he initially paid in taxes. Government taxation thereby providing both the need for the money, and the money for the need, from the combination of which the financial institutions profit at the expense of those who provided the money in the first place!*

Thus although overleveraging may, as outlined above, maximize short-term returns on investment, being, as we have seen, largely predicated upon the sale of (securitized) derivatives and so on and the capacity to insure (via credit default swaps) against downside risk, such overleveraging is correlated with *great interconnectivity between the major financial institutions*, with the consequence that when one fails it often brings down others with it, thereby restricting the future availability of the credit necessary for profitable investment. The upshot being that not only the finance industry, and investors generally, suffer, but, in a capitalist economy economic growth, and jobs, suffer along with them. Furthermore, given the current size and interconnectedness of many of our financial institutions, such failure may well result in a total market meltdown and credit freeze, which would threaten the very survival of capitalism itself! A circumstance which certainly *appears* to many to leave governments, and thus ultimately the general public, with little choice other than to underwrite the risks, and bear the consequent costs,[8] of such failure.

Although, of course, once AIG, Citigroup, Bank of America, and other financial institutions, not to mention the previously failing General Motors and Chrysler and so on, returned to profitability, so far from insisting that the government retain a financial interest and perhaps voting stock also, so that it might guide the future behavior of these companies in the interests of the public upon whose investment their survival had depended, and even profit from their future development, the same politicians, of both major political parties, who arranged for the general public to fund their bailout and provide them with working capital, immediately sought to relinquished any public stake in them. This left the financial elite, who were among the few who—as a consequence of being bailed out by the general public who were therefore left strapped for cash—could still afford to buy shares in these corporations, to profit from their recovery, and the accompanying recovery in the housing market also. It therefore came to pass that in the first year of the recovery the wealthiest 1% of the population captured 93%, the wealthiest 0.1% capturing 37%, of the value of this, largely working and middle-class financed, "recovery"[9] from a crisis that

[8] See footnote 4.

[9] "Moyers and Company," PBS broadcast, October 20 and 21, 2012. Indeed, the wealthiest 1% of *families* in the US own about 40% of all US wealth, which is to say much more than the bottom 90% who own only about 25%, while the three wealthiest *individual* US citizens (Bezos, Gates, and Buffett) own more wealth than the bottom 50% of the population! Nor is such inequality limited to the US, for as Oxfam recently reported, the world's 26 wealthiest

they (the wealthy financial elite) had, through the economic system they supported, and their risky lending strategies, had precipitated in the first place! A circumstance which further significantly exacerbated, already great, economic inequality.

Billionaires own as much wealth as the bottom half, or about 3.9 Billion, of the world's population!

CHAPTER 4

# Capitalism's Two Major Justifications Dismissed, and the Incentivized Complicity of the Bought and Paid for Politicians to Ignore, and Even Encourage, the Risky/Costly Behavior of the Economic Oligarchs

**Abstract** In *socializing*, via bailouts, *downside costs* and allowing the *privatization of upside profits*, not only does government underwrite capitalist's risking of their capital, but *militates against the optimal deployment of resources to the most efficient*, who would otherwise be victors of the neo-Darwinian struggle for survival. Furthermore, it is *labor*, *whether intellectual* (i.e. managerial, executive, design, creative, etc.) *or/and physical*, *which turns resources into valuable goods and services.* All of which raises the question as to why capitalism per se, should derive profit (at the expense of wages) from wealth production at all? While government complicity in this, and in entering into delayed or non-prosecution agreements even when the financial elite engage in the most egregious criminal behavior, raises questions of democratic accountability.

**Keywords** Risk socialization • Profit privatization • Deferred and Non-Prosecution Agreements

Now *most significantly*, the *socialization of downside risks/costs and privatization of upside profits clearly undermine the two most compelling, if not indeed the only two barely credible, arguments for capitalism*, *viz.* (1) *That*



S. Glynn, *The Economic Logic of Late Capitalism and the Inevitable Triumph of Socialism*,
https://doi.org/10.1007/978-3-030-52667-2_4

*the neo-Darwinian free market competition, supposedly characteristic of capitalism, ensures that only the fittest (in the limited sense of the most efficient) will survive and prosper, thereby promoting the optimal deployment of resources, and* (2) *That given that in the event of the failure it is the capitalist, and not society at large, who will bear the cost, the capital investment necessary for production will only be forthcoming if the risk individuals or institutions bear by investing is compensated for by their being able to profit from those investments that are successful.*

Turning to the first argument, clearly the bailing out of those businesses and financial corporations that would otherwise go under, not only rescues the inefficient but actually *promotes* them, and in so doing actually militates *against* the emergence and prosperity of the most efficient! For those corporations and financial institutions thought to be so large and/or interconnected that their individual failure might substantially threaten the system being, in consequence, effectively insured against catastrophic downside risk/cost by the promise of government bailouts, are therefore not only able to borrow money at lower rates than their smaller, would-be, competitors, but are also more willing to make riskier investments, from which they and their investors can reap greater profits. The consequence being that no matter how unfit, in the sense of inefficient or poor their judgment, these large and interconnected financial corporations will, by precisely being in a position to have the system fit them, come to dominate, as we can see them doing, an ever greater share of the market!

As for the second argument, given, as we have seen, that it is the general public who *not only* provide the investment, via savings, pension plans and taxes, which either provide or back the creation or leveraging of so much working capital, *but also*, more significantly, ultimately "backstop" or underwrite the downside risk/cost of failure, then it is ultimately not private, but on the contrary often public, capital which is at stake.[1] In light of which *it seems entirely unreasonable that the economic elite should reap the upside profits accruing to the enterprises that the general public both*

[1] While in any event, as all competent economists know, *capital*, whether liquid capital in the form of financial assets, or fixed capital investment, in, for instance, machinery, or software programs for example, is, of course, *ultimately* only stored *labor* (in the sense that it was the product of labor, whether physical or intellectual) anyway, just as the rendering—by harvesting or extraction and/or refinement and so on—of "god given" *natural resources* as usable economic resources, is also dependent on labor as is their transformation into consumer goods and services. This being, of course, the Labor Theory of Value.

*capitalize and ultimately underwrite or insure.*[2] Moreover, even more significantly, *it is clear that, to the degree that the provision of much of the capital and risk insurance ultimately falls to the general, tax paying, public, capitalists*—although not of course designers, executives, managers, and those entrepreneurs who also contribute physical or/and intellectual labor to production—*have become redundant*; it not being without irony that this redundancy is then, as a matter of fact, precisely an instance of what Schumpeter referred to (after Marx) as "creative destruction,"[3] of which neo-liberal economists, as we shall see, purport to be so enamored!

Notwithstanding this however, clearly, in light of the perverse double incentive, provided not only by the promise of high returns, but by the knowledge that if sufficiently interconnected to other financial institutions they will be bailed out, it is little wonder that the finance industry is so vehemently opposed to regulation that might *restrict* both, on the one hand overleveraging and risky, and therefore high interest, loans, and, on the other the maintenance, not to mention the creation, of the "too big to fail" size of financial institutions which ultimately ensures such bailouts![4] And capitalists have been and will continue to be successful in such opposition so long as the politicians, ostensibly charged with representing the public interest, recognize that the more under or unregulated the market, and concomitantly greater the risk of potential meltdown, the more indispensable to their wealthy campaign donors are their services in brokering the middle-class underwriting of the ensuing costs. A fact which, perversely, incentivizes these politicians to ignored or even enable the risky and even illegal practices of many of their wealthy donors in the financial

[2] Nor, of course, can it be argued that the capitalist derives a right to private profits due to management skills or design of production and/or marketing systems and so on. For, although such functions may be taken on by small entrepreneurs, they are not, in fact, functions of capital *per se*, but of intellectual labor (which capital can, and does, hire in) as is particularly obvious vis-à-vis finance capital, which, *in its purest form*, does not provide any comparable services to any *external* party, and is, concomitantly, clearly entirely parasitic!

[3] See Schumpeter, J. 1942. *Capitalism, Socialism and Democracy*, London: Routledge.

[4] Indeed, even if financial institutions per se could not rely on such government or taxpayer bailouts, their executives, who are often rewarded year to year by bonuses based on the annual or short-term performance of the stocks of the institutions they supposedly serve, would nevertheless still have every reason to embrace the very risk taking that is likely to produce long-term instability. For after all, having been handsomely rewarded when their bets pay off, if and when their institutions collapse they can always look elsewhere for future employment in the unlikely event, given their likely previous bonuses, that they continue to feel the need for any employment whatsoever!

markets. This then largely explains why the government has been so reticent to prosecute, even to the very limited degree allowed and seemingly required by the admittedly insufficient laws currently in place, the individuals who and agencies which issued mortgages to those they knew to be unqualified (an aspect of the so-called predatory lending) and/or who gave or sold bonds and derivatives with "Triple A" ratings despite the fact that they must have known they approached junk status. It also helps explains why, even in some of the most extreme, and clearly criminal, cases, where violation was both so egregious and glaringly obvious that it could not be ignored, between 2004 and the 2016 the Justice Department entered into over 500 Non-Prosecution or Deferred Prosecution Agreement with corporations. And when it had little option other than to prosecute, even in clearly criminal cases, it nevertheless largely limited itself to bringing civil, rather than criminal, prosecutions, and settled for relatively low financial penalties.

For instance while HSBC, which had a Half Trillion Dollar money laundering operation, much of it knowingly involving Latin American drug cartels, managed to get or buy itself a Deferred Prosecution for considerably less than half of 1% ($1.92 Billion, the cost of doing business) of that, J.P. Morgan Chase, determined by the US attorney in Manhattan to be guilty of two felony violations of the Bank Securities Act, was also able to buy itself a Deferred Prosecution, and paid a $2 Billion civil penalty for its cover up of Bernie Madoff's Ponzi Scheme. While even its record-breaking $13 Billion civil settlement for its part in the mortgage crisis which, along with the associated financial meltdown of 2008 wiped out almost $13 Trillion in household wealth, pales into insignificance when compared to the greater than $233 Billion Net Interest Income and the greater than $232 Billion Non-Interest Income it derived over the 5 years from 2008 to 2012! The one glaring exception to such prosecutorial reticence of course being Bernie Madoff, who unlike so many other financiers, whose actions effect mainly middle-class mortgagees, investors, and taxpayers, actually had the temerity to rip off the top 1%!

Thus, in return for lax government financial regulation and enforcement, and the brokering of the middle-class underwriting of the concomitant risk and cost of such laxity and consequent infusion of cheap capital, the financial institutions and the economic elite continue to contribute generously to the politicians' election funds, thereby helping them to get re-elected and continue to do their bidding! Indeed *not unlike the structurally parallel arrangement by which politicians ensure that billions of taxpayers' dollars are spent on subsidizing the oil, gas, and agribusiness corporations, which then use a proportion of this money to back lobbying, political advertising and the financing of the political campaigns of candidates who, when elected or re-elected, will ensure the continuation of such corporate welfare, here also we have a form of legalized corruption by which the economic elite and their financial institutions turn their wealth into political influence and their political influence back into ever greater wealth!*[5]

[5] Thus, it has come to pass that the top 1% of *individuals* in the US population owns more *wealth* than the bottom 90% of the US population combined. A financial elite whose interests are often entirely at odds with the average member of the middle classes who may, after a lifetime of work, have a few hundred thousand, or perhaps even a couple of a million, dollars of savings tucked away in a 401(k) or 403(b) retirement account; an elite who, due to their far greater resources, are clearly able, as we can see, to influence the political system and market regulation in their favor, at the expense of the middle classes.

CHAPTER 5

# Supply Side Stimulus: The Bailing Out of the Finance Industry, and It's Ensuing Self-Dealing Slowing Down Recovery

**Abstract** Instead of government bailout money being used to rescue those "underwater" with their mortgages and otherwise buoy up consumer demand, much was invested by the finance industry in itself, while much of the cost of the bailout *ultimately* fell upon the general public, further depressing demand. This resulted in the bankruptcy of many small businesses, further mortgage foreclosures, and further dampening of demand, accompanied by reduction in property taxes and so on, the reduction in spending by, and in some cases bankruptcy of, local government, further unemployment, and so on. While tellingly post 2009 the financial bubble, boosted by the supply of bailout money to the finance industry, and the return of inadequately collateralized financial instruments, resulted in an enormous stock market boom.

**Keywords** Dampening demand • Financial bubble • Increased share prices

Despite all we have seen in the previous chapter regarding fraudulent financial activity, and the redundancy of capitalists per se, all this might have been overlooked so long as the economy, upon which they are parasitic, had also continued to deliver for everyone else as well; that is if the increased wealth of the capitalist elite, and even the rising inequality, had



S. Glynn, *The Economic Logic of Late Capitalism and the Inevitable Triumph of Socialism*,
https://doi.org/10.1007/978-3-030-52667-2_5

also been accompanied by an increase in, or at least the maintenance of, the standard of living of the working and middle classes. However, well over a decade after the start of the Great Recession the US economy still had a lackluster growth rate, which even prior to the Covid-19 pandemic was struggling to maintain 2%, an *actual* unemployment rate somewhere around 11%[1] and a combined unemployment and underemployment rate of about 15%. But why? Why, given TARP and QE, and the concomitant lowering of interest rates, or the cost of borrowing, that ostensibly accompanies such an increase in the *Supply* of money—not to mention the threat of inflation, and the concomitant devaluation of "money" resulting from such an increase, which should provide an additional incentive to invest—has recovery in the "real" economy been so sluggish and limited?

Because although in theory an increase in the supply of money to financial institutions, and the concomitant reduction in interest rates should, as previously mentioned, stimulate *both investment on the Supply side*, and consumer credit backed *spending on the Demand side*, not only did the *cost* of TARP and QE fall largely upon middle-class taxpayers[2] even as the increased supply of money put downward pressure on actual and expected *returns* on fixed rate or/and money market financial savings and pension plans related thereto, therefore putting considerable downward pressure on demand, but much of what US corporations received through financial institutions they invested overseas. An *outsourcing* of production, and thus

[1] The official unemployment figure, prior to the Covid-19 pandemic, of around 3.5% owed much to the fact that many of the 25 Million or so under or unemployed, having been unemployed for a considerable time, had either given up looking, and thus fallen out of the labor market, or, having become ineligible over such a long period for further financial benefits, though still looking for work, saw no reason to continue to register with the government as doing so. Moreover, unlike more traditional jobs, many of the jobs in the new, so-called gig, economy, like that of Uber drivers for example, lack pensions, health care, or indeed any other benefits, and are precariously dependent upon the interests or whims of the employer.

[2] While certainly by running a deficit, it is possible to defer these costs, in the long run of course they become repayable with considerable accrued interest (again to the considerable advantage of the wealthy who can finance such deficits, as the politicians who approve such deficits are well aware) as many middle-class taxpayers know, as evidenced by the call by some of them, to balance the budget, and by their reluctant to take on further private debt. A general pessimism which further reduces demand.

of not just physical labor but technical and other services (of which more later) that *put downward pressure on domestic wages and employer funding of pension and healthcare benefits also.* All of which, together with the reduction in the value of housing assets due to the bursting of the inflationary bubble in the housing market which *in the minds of most* was the cause of the financial meltdown in the first place, has put enormous downside pressure on the *Demand* for goods and services necessary if such investment is to be profitable.

And as if all this were not, in and of itself, sufficient to account for the sluggish recovery of the economy, the problem was further exacerbated by the fact that, mindful of the fact that their previous predatory mortgage lending and lax mortgage borrowing requirements were widely regarded as the cause of the initial financial meltdown, financial institutions were, by invoking this belief, able to justify their reluctance to refinance, at lower interest rates, those mortgages which, as a consequence of the bursting of the property market bubble, were underwater. Indeed, their insisting for the most part that only those mortgagees who were NOT underwater could refinance at the new, lower, rates,[3] resulted in large numbers of mortgage holders being foreclosed on. A similar rational being used by them to justify their reluctance to lend to all but the most qualified new would-be borrowers. Decisions which, as the large amounts of money left on the sidelines un-invested by them and (temporarily) not generating any returns clearly indicate, were not entirely unmotivated by the recognition that the housing glut that increased foreclosures, together with unnecessarily demanding new mortgage eligibility requirements, would drive down house prices to rock bottom, so that, when future recovery was on the horizon, these financial institutions would have sufficient funds that they themselves would be in a position to hoover up large quantities of housing at rock bottom prices. Housing which they could then rent out at what, given the large numbers of those who, as a consequence of defaulting on their

[3] While it is true that in the US banks and other financial institutions eventually, at the direction of the federal government, somewhat reluctantly begun, largely for what appear to be mainly cosmetic or public relations reasons, allowing a few US homeowners who were underwater to renegotiate their mortgage contracts so that they could take advantage of the lower interest rates, this only affected a very small percentage of the approximately 17 Million US underwater households, and was thus clearly a case of "too little, too late" to make any real difference to the market overall.

previous mortgages could no longer obtain mortgages and were therefore force into rented accommodation, were consequently inflated rates, until such time as prices recovered, and they could sell at much higher prices! Reasons for a reluctance to bail out defaulting mortgages to which must be added the financial institutions' realization that many, left with negative equity in their homes and still required to continue paying high interest on their mortgages and home equity loans, recognizing the adverse consequences to their credit ratings and so on of defaulting on their mortgages, would—if they still had other assets, such as job security and future earnings, that could be wrung out of them—as a last resort, be prepared to turn to these very financial institutions for credit card and other forms of high interest borrowing.

All of this, of course, had the entirely foreseeable consequence, not only of reducing consumer *demand* for goods and services, but of reducing collectable property taxes, and thus the revenue stream *to*, and therefore employment *by*, local government, resulting in a number of cases in the actual bankruptcy of local and city governments.[4] All of which depressed demand for goods and services still further. This then led to the bankruptcy of many small businesses, adding to the unemployment rolls, which in addition to further reducing tax revenues as well as the demand for goods and services, resulted in even more mortgage foreclosures, a drop in property values and more underwater mortgages, which resulted in a further decline in the *demand* for goods and services, the bankruptcy of more small businesses, more unemployment and so on and on; a great "unwinding" which served only to deepen and prolong the recession.

Nor, most revealingly—despite arguing, when lobbying for tax breaks and subsidies for wealthy investors and their businesses, that *Demand* would, as a consequence "*trickle down*"—were the advocates of *Supply side* economics, absent the *preexistence* of rigorous *Demand*, prepared, even with such tax incentives and subsidies, to invest in the *Supply* side; which

[4]These included, but were no means limited to Detroit MI, San Bernardino CA, Harrisburg PA, Stockton CA, and so on.

is to say in those businesses in the "*real*"[5]economy,[6] which had gone into debt as a result of the initial economic downturn, but could, like the underwater homeowner, have survived by refinancing their debts at lower rates. *Indeed, facing the previously analyzed downturn in demand in the real economy, and recognizing that in face of the fact that the investment capital provided by the government to them was, if not derived from, then ultimately underwritten by, public taxation which, as per the previously mentioned "shell game" stimulated public demand for credit, the finance industry realized that it could make far greater profits by investing in itself. The consequence of which being many companies buying up their own shares, and an unprecedented surge of mergers and acquisitions within the finance industry, which resulted, of course, in an inflation of finance industry share prices which not only enormously increased the wealth of those senior directors and managers of financial corporations with substantial company stock-holdings or stock options, but additionally delivered to them large, performance linked, bonuses.*

For instance, Wells Fargo acquired Wachovia, Bank of America acquired Merrill Lynch and Countrywide, and J.P. Morgan acquired Bear Stearns and Washington Mutual. A situation which, in addition to the great benefit derived by those wealthy enough to have sizable holdings therein, also had the perverse effect of making such institutions, already regarded as

[5] The distinction I wish to draw here is with the *financial* economy, the *real* economy producing material goods and non-financial services, without which the "wealth" or "money" generated by the entirely parasitic financial economy would have no *real* value, as it would not be exchangeable for anything except other "money." A distinction I would have thought to be glaringly obvious had I not attended a symposium at The Hamptons Institute (in East Hampton, Long Island, New York) entitled "America's Economic Future: A Bipartisan Conversation" where, despite its title, not one of the four "eminent" panelists, nor any of the audience who questioned them, thought to say anything about the real economy but, rather, spoke only of regulatory oversight of banks, hedge funds, accounting practices and the like! In this context, it is noteworthy that the financial sector of the US economy, which generated approximately 15% of corporate profits in 1985, was, by 2008, responsible for approximately 40% of such profits! (Turner, C. 2012. Eco-Geo. *The Nation*, December 17, 2012, p. 44).

[6] Which, given the fact that as a consequence of the recession there already existed many under or unutilized, non-liquid or fixed, capital assets or underutilized production capacity, that could readily be brought back into service if, as and when, demand picked up, such investment in the real economy would not have itself resulted in any great increase, albeit *indirect*, in demand either.

"too big and interconnected to fail" even more so.[7] *While other financial institutions often collected interest on this government provided—and thus if not tax payer derived then tax payer underwritten—money by (and I kid you not) lending it back to the government that provided it! Interest which, like the initial loan, is, of course, ultimately paid for by the taxpayer who provided the funds for, or underwrote, the government loan in the first place!*

Now despite the fact that such strategies have drawn money away from investment in the real (or non-financial) economy, and consequently slowed, and ultimately inhibited, a full recovery, they have met with nothing more than the faintest, ineffectual, murmur of protest from the alleged political "representatives" of *the people; which is to say the supposed representatives of the general population which has underwritten and—via public taxation and an increase in the National Debt and unfunded mandates (of which more later)—borne and will continue to bear the cost of, such financial transactions.* While given the consequently lackluster recovery in the "real" economy it is evident that the well over 4.5 fold increase in stock market values (The Dow Jones Industrial Stock Index bottomed out at 6443 on March 6, 2009, and topped out at 29,551 on February 12, 2020) since the meltdown and prior to the Covid-19 pandemic's effect, was in large part the product of such financial engineering. The boosting of the money supply by QE, and sharp increases in the National Debt, together with low interest rates, not to mention the return of often inadequately collateralized financial instruments and their derivatives thus clearly being the way in which the finance industry again begun re-inflating the financial bubble!

[7] The largest banks have increased in size by approximately 30% since the onset of the financial crisis.

CHAPTER 6

# The Disaster of Austerity as a Road to Recovery; "Democracy," Understood as a Source of Legitimation to be Suspended by the Financial Oligarchs in the Name of Austerity

**Abstract** While the US was able to delay reducing its deficit, and even to increase its debt, the ECB and the IMF demanded Eurozone economies suffering significantly from the Great Recession immediately reduce government spending and begin paying down their debt. Demand killing austerity which caused further economic contraction, often resulting in the decline in GDP being greater than the reduction in government spending. Their national debts, therefore becoming an ever-greater percentage of their shrinking GDP, made it increasingly difficult for these economies to pay them off, occasioning the replacing of democratically elected leaders in countries such as Italy and Greece, by financial technocrats. This in contrast to the US, where the political class, having long subordinated the national interest to those of the corporate oligarchs, faced no such challenge from their owners.

**Keywords** Eurozone austerity • Fiscal multiplier • Democracy suspended • Legitimation crisis • Financial oligarchs

If things have been bad for the real economy in the US, they have been even worse for many in Western Europe in general, where at least nine



S. Glynn, *The Economic Logic of Late Capitalism and the Inevitable Triumph of Socialism*,
https://doi.org/10.1007/978-3-030-52667-2_6

economies contracted,[1] and in the so-called PIGS (Portugal, Ireland, Greece, and Spain) of the Euro Zone in particular. For unlike the US, which has been able to delay reducing its annual *deficits* and paying down its *debt*[2]—which had they not been delayed would have reduced the availability of money and/or credit, thereby depressing demand even further—until such time as a real recovery is underway, while at the same time increasing the supply of money through QE, the PIGS have not been permitted to do either. Rather they have had to follow the dictates of the International Monetary Fund (IMF) and the European Central Bank (ECB), which controls the money supply in the Euro Zone. And these institutions insist that as a precondition of being lent money to recapitalize their failing financial institutions, and under threat of massive hikes in interest rates due to the perceived threat of default, these economies immediately begin paying down their debt by bringing their annual deficit into surplus. Facing many of the same demand depressing circumstances as the US, and additionally being unable to embark upon QE, this they have only been able to do by instituting the most severe austerity measures. Austerity measures which increase tax rates while cutting government spending, and thus public sector employment and pay, public benefits (e.g. welfare, pensions, and even the publically funded healthcare long emblematic of the civilized world) and government-funded, but privately contracted, public works and services, consequently depressing demand still further.

All of which had the entirely predictable effect of plunging these economies into deep (in some cases of the order of over 20%) and prolonged recession, resulting in massive job losses (e.g., unemployment typically being around 25% overall, and toping 60% for those under 25 years in Spain for example). Job losses which have, in addition to the decline in tax revenues from corporations resulting from recession, resulted in declining tax *revenues* from workers, while fueling demand for benefits, which have jointly added to the deficit, requiring further, demand killing, austerity, and consequently the loss of yet more jobs, and so on. While in addition to the great hardship that this inflicts upon so much of the population, it has often resulted in *the decline in Gross Domestic Product (GDP) being*

[1] Greider, W. 2012. The Fed and the Silence of the Left. *The Nation*. (Nov. 26) p. 18.

[2] The *deficit* is, of course, the (annual) negative difference between the value of (both visible and invisible) exports and imports, while the *debt* is the (year on year) accumulation of such annual deficits.

*greater than the reduction in government spending*, the *fiscal multiplier (or former as a ratio of the latter, by which it is divided) being in many cases greater than 1; which is to say the decrease in the total wealth generated being greater than the reduction in the deficit, which becomes, in consequence, a greater percentage of the GDP, making it more difficult to pay down.* Thus in Greece for example, despite a marked reduction in government spending, the even more rapidly shrinking economy that this helped bring about resulted in public sector debt increasing from 144% of GDP in 2010 to 170% by 2012.[3] Indeed noting that fiscal "multipliers have actually been in the 0.9 to 1.7 range,"[4] the IMF, a long-time advocate of such austerity programs, acknowledged at its October 2012 meeting in Tokyo that the application of such programs to many of the countries of Southern Europe had "been counterproductive, undermining economic growth and increasing rather than bringing down public debt ratios,"[5] and consequently even started to ease up on such policies. But not before George Papandreou, the Prime Minister of Greece (from whence "democracy" is widely regarded as having originated) was, as a consequence of his audacious suggestion that the proposed terms and conditions of the financial bailout of Greece might be put to a democratic referendum, replaced by unelected former ECB Vice President Lucas Papademos, just as democratically elected Italian Prime Minister Silvio Berlusconi was replaced by unelected (EU) technocrat Mario Monti. Democracy thus being revealed as no more than a convenient way, under normal circumstances, of avoiding a "legitimation crisis," only to be tolerated by the *dictatorship of the financial oligarchs* for so long as it makes no significant difference to their interests. A lesson that Alexis Tsipras and Yanis Varoufakis (ex-prime minister and ex-finance minister respectively of the subsequently democratically elected Syriza government) soon learned!

In the US of course, where "What's good for General Motors is (purportedly) good for the USA," which is to say a country where national interest has long since been openly and explicitly recognized as being eclipsed by, and indeed seen by many as rightly subordinated to, corporate interests, and where, concomitantly, as we have seen, capitalism has infiltrated the political class which it now holds captive largely via campaign financing, there was therefore never any need for a financial oligarch

[3] Robinson, A. 2012. Euro Austerity Under Fire. *The Nation.* (Dec. 10) p. 8.

[4] Ibid., quoting the IMF's *Economic Outlook* report.

[5] Ibid.

backed coup, as there was never any question of the political class challenging the corporate interests that it so adeptly represents in the first place. Thus George W. Bush's Federal Reserve chairman Ben Bernanke had no difficulty in persuading the captive political class that having "stared into the abyss" and been confronted with a vision of the permanent collapse of capitalism, there was no alternative—except socialism of course, which didn't bear thinking about—other than to supply those corporations, which might otherwise have been forced to part with their ill-gotten gains and thus into bankruptcy, with obscene amounts of money in order to pay off some of the enormous debt they had incurred as a consequence of their reckless pursuit of short-term profits. Money which, instead of being immediately directed to finance a genuine recovery in the *real economy*, which would have benefited the general population, was of course, as already noted, used almost exclusively in the interests of bankers and other financiers to *finance the recovery of the financial economy and, through the aforementioned mergers and acquisitions of financial institutions, and the buyback of publically owned shares in their institutions, to drive up share prices, as well as to hoover up housing at rock bottom prices; all of which is to say to further enrich themselves.*

However, although the bankruptcies of a number of financial institutions might have set capitalism back, it most surely would not, contra Bernanke's assertion, have portended its immediate, much less, at that stage at least, its permanent, collapse. Unless, of course, the general public had got wind of the wholly parasitic nature of finance capitalism, and therefore rightly conclude that it was not only totally dispensable, but actually contributing to their economic malaise. An entirely unlikely outcome in light of the corporate infiltration and control of the "mainstream media"—which is largely composed of free standing corporations, or owned and controlled by larger "parent" corporations,[6] and ultimately, in

[6]Thus while Disney's ownership of ABC is an immediately understandable example of vertical integration, in that Disney may produce the programming that ABC broadcasts, recent owners of CBS, Westinghouse, manufactures of nuclear and other power plants, military aircraft, navy power units and the like, and NBC owners General Electric, whose interests include finance, oil and gas, military weaponry and the like, seem to have no immediately identifiable common interests with the broadcast corporations they own. However, by controlling the media they clearly exert enormous influence over the information and its interpretation readily available to the general public, and thus over cultural norms, public opinion, and consequently over the *manufacturing* of consent around government or "public" policy. An influence which in determining the social, cultural, political, and economic "climate" or

either case, by the economic elite—and of the "education" system.[7] While even if the general public were indeed to become aware of all of this, given the capture of the political class by the financial elite, and its concomitant capacity to manipulate, and, as we have seen, replace democratically elected officials, and even democracy itself, short of a revolution nothing much would likely change, and it would still be, as currently in Greece, business as usual!

world view [*weltanschauung*] in which they operate, is clearly of the upmost significance to their non-media operations and their profitability!

[7] Thus, even publically funded educational institutions, increasingly governed by trustees and regents and so on selected almost exclusively from the business community, are—as evidenced by former Wisconsin Governor Scott Walker's attempt to replace the "search for truth" and "improvement of the human condition," which were traditionally the missions of the University of Wisconsin system, with that of "meet(ing) the state's workforce needs"—under mounting pressure to look to the corporate world to inform them what it is that they should be teaching in order to remain "relevant." While students increasingly perceive institutions of higher learning, not, primarily, as places where they may *receive an education*, try to understand interesting facts and ideas, and raise, and perhaps try to settle, significant issues, but rather as places where they may *get a degree*, understood merely as a *credential* facilitating their entry into the job market.

CHAPTER 7

# Demand Side Stimulus: The Democratic Socialist Alternative

**Abstract** Instead of allowing financial corporations to benefit further from a crisis that they precipitated and profited from for so long by providing them with taxpayer funded bailouts, a truly representative, democratic government would have surely bailed out those underwater in their mortgages, and small businesses bankrupted by the recession, and facilitated the renegotiation or refinancing, at lower interest rates, of home equity loans, credit card and student debt, and so on. This would have stabilized house prices, maintained property tax revenues to local government, enabled businesses to continue employing, and providing taxable pay and so on to, their employees, and generally contributed to ***demand side stimulus*** that would have limited the recession and speeded recovery. A solution which as well as being ***pragmatically*** efficacious would have been ***morally*** equitable.

**Keywords** Demand side stimulus • Pragmatically efficacious • Morally equitable

But what if, despite being largely "informed" as they are, by corporately owned mainstream media, and "educated" by institutions which actively seek to subordinate whatever other function they may have traditionally served, to the research and job training demands of the capitalist economy, the general public were to become aware of the fact that they are only allowed to participate in the economy to the degree that they



S. Glynn, *The Economic Logic of Late Capitalism and the Inevitable Triumph of Socialism*,
https://doi.org/10.1007/978-3-030-52667-2_7

are needed in order to make profits for the financial elite? And what if they recognized that even when the wealthy do not go so far as to suspend democracy, they nevertheless, via campaign financing, act as a *Selectorate* which, as such, circumscribe the power of the *Electorate*? And what if they further recognized that even, if as and when, the odd, perhaps crowd funded, candidate, was nevertheless able to mount a significant campaign, the corporate owned and controlled mainstream media, together with lavishly funded opponents, could, by framing issues and providing self-serving representations and interpretations of such candidates, their motives, and their policies, largely neutralize—or should they gain office circumscribe the effective power of—those who threatened their interests?

Granted it might be a bit of a stretch to imagine that, even were they to ever be made aware of what we have seen to be the largely redundant, not to say parasitic, nature of finance capital, the general public, would immediately institute a Socialist revolution. And not least because—notwithstanding the fact that socialism, like capitalism and communism are essentially ***economic*** systems, while democracy and dictatorship as ***political*** systems, lie on an entirely independent axis—the general public have been so systematically misinformed as to believe that capitalism is necessarily democratic (cf. Hitler's Germany, Pinochet's Chile, Batista's Cuba, Saudi Arabia, Bahrain) or even productive of affluence (cf. Democratic Republic of Congo, Haiti, Niger, Ethiopia) and socialism is necessarily autocratic and poor (cf. Holland, Sweden, Finland, Denmark, Norway). Nevertheless surely it is not unrealistic to suppose that they would work toward political reform aimed at ensuring that instead of they and their political "representatives" and institutions conforming themselves to the dictates of, and thus serving the interests of, national and transnational corporations, financial markets, and international financial institutions such as the International Monetary Fund (IMF) and the European Central Bank (ECB), rather that these corporations, markets, and institutions, not to mention the political system, should be so configured as to serve ***their*** (the general public's) interests. For indeed, to co-opt a slogan of the "Occupy" movement "This is what (a functioning) democracy (would) look(s) like."

Thus a functioning democracy truly representative of the will of the people would surely not begin by implementing ***demand suppressing austerity*** measures, aimed at already relatively impecunious homeowners, taxpayers, public education, healthcare, pension, welfare, unemployment and other public benefit and recipients, while at the same time providing *corporate welfare*, a.k.a. "*Supply Side* stimulus" in the form of vast quantities of entirely free finance capital and low interest (0.5% or less) loans. Loans which, in light of suppressed demand in the "real" economy, the recipients mainly invested in themselves and for their own profit. Indeed, so far from allowing corporations and financial institutions to exploit the crisis that was the Great Recession *which*, let us not forget, ***they precipitated*** *and profit from* for so long, by using much of the money—financed or backed by taxpayers, or/and at the expense of prudent small savers—provided to them, to facilitate share buybacks, acquisitions and mergers in the finance industry itself, and acquisition of housing at rock bottom prices, thereby enriching themselves *at the general taxpayer and homeowners expense*, a truly representative government would surely have adopting something like a "Keynesian," or *Demand Side*, solution. Which is to say it would have insisted that the increase in the money supply be used to bail out hard pressed homeowners, including those with underwater mortgages, and to enable them, and other individuals burdened with home equity and credit card debt and student loans and so on, and other, increasingly unserviceable debt, to renegotiate or refinance that debt at lower interest rates. Individuals who, instead of defaulting on their mortgages, and other debts, would then have continued to pay them down, and would continue paying property taxes, thereby maintained a robust revenue stream to local government, and therefore employment of, and pensions and other benefits for, *public sector employees*, as well as for employees of private contractors of services to local government. A circumstance which, by stabilizing domestic real estate prices, and enabling widespread escape from unserviceable debt burden, as well as financing employment, would have helped maintain, if not stimulate, *demand* for goods and services in the real economy. And thus removing any excuse for not investing in this real economy, financial institutions would, rather than investing in themselves, have been required to direct such taxpayer provided and/or backed provision of finance capital, to low interest loans to typically smaller job-generating businesses in the private sector of the *real* economy; businesses which, even though in some cases indebted due to a failure to anticipate the financial meltdown, nevertheless showed themselves to be (otherwise) potentially capable of generating a positive cash flows once demand stabilized. Businesses which would not only have been able to continue to pay their employees, and help finance their pensions and other benefits, but to pay business taxes; taxes which in conjunction with those paid by their, *private sector*, employees, would, in addition to helping to finance both local and federal government spending, and the employment, pensions and other benefits of their *public sector* employees, could also potentially fund healthcare for all, as well as welfare and other benefits to those citizens who nevertheless still found themselves unemployed or otherwise in need of help due to the financial meltdown.

Such policies would then have resulted in a rapid upturn in demand, which those who would have continued to be employed would consequently have been in a position to supply with real goods and services. A virtuous cycle which would have fueled much more rapid recovery and growth in *the real economy; the real economy, without which profits from the financial economy would be valueless.* And should anyone be skeptical of this *demand side* analysis, they have only to recollect, as we previously saw, that it was hardly lack of a *supply* of investment capital, but lack of consumer *demand*, together with the perception that this was unlikely to increase significantly anytime soon, which was clearly largely responsible for dampening the finance industry's enthusiasm for such investment, and which consequently held back a potentially much more robust and rapid recovery. A conclusion further evidenced by the fact that, slow as the US recovery in the *real* economy, even prior to the coronavirus pandemic, was, it was certainly quicker and more robust than that of those European nations subjected to sharper cuts in government spending, and/or greater austerity, than the US, but much slower than that of China, whose government-funded investment in infrastructure, and thus in jobs in the real economy, and the increasing prosperity of the general population which this resulted in, enabled them to maintain, stimulate, and even increase *domestic* demand even as foreign demand fell drastically.

Not that understanding the importance of maintaining *demand* in this manner is completely foreign to US capitalism, for it was, after all, none other than Henry Ford who, when asked why he paid his workers well above the prevailing market rate for their labor replied that he did so in order that they could afford to buy the vehicles they were producing; a strategy only possible in a competitive free market by virtue of Ford's comparatively high productivity[1] thanks to the utilization of a production line, whose efficiency was enhanced by Taylorism.[2] A lesson in demand stimulation which FDR was to learn from Keynes, and apply in responding to the Great Depression by ramping up government investment in wage boosting projects. Government investment which—although temporally trimmed in the middle of the Great Depression, when premature concern about the US national debt resulted in ill-advised cutbacks in government

[1] The term productivity referring not to the overall number or level of goods and/or services being produced, but to *efficiency* of the productive process, which is to say the ratio of the value of the product or output to or over the cost of the input, which, other things being equal, is of course generally a function of the efficiency of the technology and labor being employed in production.

[2] Fredric Winslow Taylor pioneered many management, organizational, and production theories.

spending which produced the "double dip" of 1937–38—together with the resumption of government spending during WWII, particularly on the *production* of weapons,[3] (when concern about the nation's security trumped concern about the national debt) eventually helped usher in the US post-war boom! And thereafter it was precisely the superiority of the post-WWII US economy—which had not only ramped up production to supply the Allies, but had escaped wartime devastation of technological infrastructure endured by other leading industrial nations with which it would otherwise had to compete—which, relieving the US from significant wage and benefit restrictions, resulted in a "virtuous circle" of *demand-driven* growth of unprecedented duration. Such *domestic demand-driven* growth being further boosted by Marshall Aid and otherwise financed *foreign demand*, from a war torn Western Europe and Japan, for the capital equipment needed to help rebuild their economies.

However, as a consequence of being prohibited by post-WWII terms of treaty from investing significantly in the production of weapons and other forms of military technology, West Germany and Japan in particular, whose investment was therefore focused upon other forms of productive industrial technology, increasingly became economic competitors, thereby eroding the premium wages and other, demand sustaining, benefits, that had spurred post-war US economic growth. A circumstance which was to lay bare both the **moral** and **ontological dilemmas** facing *laissez-faire capitalism*.

[3]Weapons which, so far from adding to the supply of consumer goods threatening to overwhelm the demand of the US public, were shipped, on credit, to the Allies, leaving the US workers with sufficient money in their pockets to buy the expanding supply of consumer goods produced to satisfy this demand. While the Marshall Plan helped ensured continuing demand from a heavily indebted Europe, as, similarly, did aid to Japan.

CHAPTER 8

# Capitalism's Moral and Ontological Dilemmas: Competition, the Inevitably Exploitative Response, and the Crisis of Overproduction

**Abstract** If capitalists are to survive in a *truly* competitive free market they must maximize productivity or efficiency, which is to say the ratio of output to input. Consequently, wages must be minimized, while any health care, education, housing, and other social benefits, insofar as they do not substantially boost productivity, being therefore at the expense of efficiency, are necessarily precluded. Furthermore, turning from capitalism's *moral* dilemma to its *ontological* dilemma, *increased* efficiency or *productivity*, *necessary if it is to remain competitive*, in driving down wages and benefits, and driving up production, *inevitably precipitates a crisis of overproduction* in that the economic demand for goods and services is overwhelmed by the supply, *thereby threatening profitability*. A dialectical contradiction between competitiveness and profitability portending capitalism's inevitable collapse.

**Keywords** Moral dilemma • Ontological dilemma • Crisis of overproduction • Dialectical contradiction

Turning now then to the ***moral and ontological*** *dilemmas of free-market or competitive capitalism*, and beginning with the former; absent effective competition from foreign economies, capitalists in the US were able to pay their workforce premium wages and other benefits, resulted in a "virtuous circle" of *demand-driven* growth. However, once faced with *competition*,



S. Glynn, *The Economic Logic of Late Capitalism and the Inevitable Triumph of Socialism*,
https://doi.org/10.1007/978-3-030-52667-2_8

if individual competitors are to survive, production costs, including wages, pensions, and other welfare benefits, must be driven down, and production driven up. *This increasing productivity—or exploitation as many would regard it—being the very efficiency* that economic neo-liberals insist is capitalism's saving grace, and therefore the justification for free-market or *laissez-faire* competition.

Thus so far from being able to promote *general economic wellbeing, and the associated social, wellbeing*—which insofar as they tend to be positively correlated with *the sum total of human happiness*, are normally regarded by Utilitarians and those of their ilk as generally morally good, and thus as standing in contrast to exploitation, which, tending to be negatively correlated thereto is normally regarded by Utilitarians, as indeed by Deontologists also, as morally objectionable[1]—*other things being equal,*[2] *competitive capitalism is structurally precluded from incurring any expenditures other than those which will maximize productivity. A circumstance which will put downward pressure, not only on wages, but, upon any and all expenditure on, or investment in, pensions, healthcare, education, housing, and other social benefits which do not boost economic productivity to the point where they result in greater profit than they cost. In which case, so far from any economically non-productive benefits that the workforce, or indeed society at large, has derived, being a testament to the social utility of free-market capitalist competition, such benefits are instantiations of capitalism's non-productive or/and uncompetitive inefficiencies.*

Nor does the fact that the provision of such benefits can, as for instance with private health care and education, also be turned into capitalist enterprises effect this equation. For not only, in such circumstances, can demand for them still only be financed at the expense of the efficiency or productivity of the initial enterprises, but they too, if they are to survive *laissez-faire* or free-market capitalism competition, will also be subject to the same dictates of competitive productivity.

Turning now then to the less obvious, but arguably more significant, **ontological dilemma**. This is constituted by a tension, or perhaps we had

[1] Thus following John Stuart Mill and Jeremy Bentham, Utilitarians are Teleologists which is to say those who judge acts to be moral or immoral on the basis of their consequences, which in the case of Utilitarians is specifically to the degree to which they add to, or subtract from, the "*sum total of human happiness,*" while Deontologists such as Immanuel Kant, to give but one example, regards certain acts as intrinsically moral or immoral regardless of their consequences or outcome.

[2] Such as the ability of each to produce goods of the same or equivalent *sort* or/and *quality*.

better say a ***contradiction*, at the very heart of capitalism**, which threatens its very existence. A contradiction identified and extensively analyzed well over a century and a half ago, by Karl Marx. *Now as just noted, survival in a competitive and transparent free market requires production costs, or inputs, be driven down, and production, or outputs, driven up; this maximization of productivity or efficiency being much vaunted by economic neo-conservatives as the justification for laissez-faire capitalism. However, insofar as demand stimulating wages and benefits are a major—if not in accordance with the Labor Theory of Value*[3] *ultimately the only—expense of production, this increased efficiency, requiring, as it therefore does, the driving down of wages, and thus of aggregate demand, undermines the previously analyzed "virtuous circle" of demand-driven economic growth, eventually making it impossible for the general public to afford the increase in goods and services they are producing. An intrinsic* ***"dialectical contradiction,"*** *which—in addition to standing as a stark refutation of economist Adam Smith's contention that an invisible or hidden hand will ensure that each, in pursuing their own individual self-interest, would thereby maximize the sum total of self-interests*[4]*—inevitably results, as Marx foresaw, in what he called a* ***"Crisis of Overproduction,"*** *resulting in Capitalism's ultimate demise.*

[3] See Chapter 4, footnote 1.

[4] A standard refutation of Smith's view is, of course, among others, Garrett Harding's "The Tragedy of the Commons," (Science, Vol. 162, No 3859, Dec. 1968) although a perhaps more immediately obvious example would be the competitive fishing of diminishing stocks of fish. Thus, aware of the diminution of stocks of fish due to overfishing, it would, in a *competitive* (economic) system be in my *individual* self-interest to catch as many fish as quickly as possible, before they all disappeared, as so too would it be in everybody else's *individual competitive* self-interest to do the same. This then would result, if not in the extinction, then at least in the severe and precipitous reduction, of the stocks of fish, to the mutual disadvantage of all. Although alternatively, recognizing the holistic logic of social/economic interactions, we may each declined to act in this *competitive* manner, but rather agreed to *cooperate* by taking only a limited quota in an attempt to enable the stocks to replenish themselves, to the mutual benefit of all. An argument that, by analogy, clearly extends to *capitalist competition*, in that if each enterprise *competes* against all others this puts downward pressure on aggregated wages, and thus on aggregate demand, thereby threatening the profitability, not to mention the survival, of all. While if alternatively, again in recognition the holistic logic of social interactions, we abandoned such *individualistic, capitalist, competition* in favor of mutual or *communal, social or socialistic cooperation*, then we would be in a position to ensure that each worker was sufficiently well paid, that in aggregate they could afford the goods that they produced. However, in effectively thereby giving the workers "the full value of their productive labor"—including, of course the intellectual labor of technological innovation, and production management and so on—necessary if they were to

To explicate the same point further. *On the one hand, in order to* ***survive*** *in a free-market, capitalists need to be* ***competitive****. This requires that they hold down, and even reduce, the cost of production, which—other things*, such as the cost of capital, natural resources and transport, and worker productivity as well as technological innovation[5] being relatively equal between competitors—*means holding down the cost of labor, including wages, pensions, and other welfare benefits. But in order to* ***survive*** *capitalism also needs to be* ***profitable****, and this requires robust economic* ***demand****, which requires robust wage and/or other benefits; expenses that, by increasing the cost of production, thereby threaten to undermine this* ***profitability****, and thus capitalism's* ***survival.*** *In other words if it is to* ***survive*** *capitalism needs to be both* ***competitive*** *and* ***profitable.*** *However* ***other things being equal****, in order to be* ***competitive*** *it must hold down wages, which depresses aggregate demand, thereby threatening its* ***profitability****, while in order to* ***profitable*** *it must stimulate demand, which requires raising wages, thereby threatening its* ***competitiveness.***

be able to purchase all the goods they produced, we would, in doing so, concomitantly be abolishing profits, and thus capitalism, in favor of socialism, or even communism.

[5] Of which more later.

CHAPTER 9

# The Crisis of Overproduction Deferred by Credit, the Consequent Growth of the Finance Industry and the Housing Bubble, and Its Bursting

**Abstract** The *crisis of overproduction*, temporarily ameliorated by *credit*, mainly in the form of mortgages, boosted demand for, and thus the price of, housing. This brought speculative investors into the market, further increasing housing's value, against which households could leverage secondary mortgages and collateralize further borrowing. This rendered not only the *financial* sector of the economy, but the *real* sector producing concrete goods and non-financial services, increasingly profitable. However, recognizing that speculatively fueled increase in housing prices rendered them increasingly unaffordable to potential occupants, upon whose demand prices *ultimately* depended, investors rushed to sell, glutting the housing market, leaving many householders underwater, and unwilling or/and unable to service the secondary mortgages and other credit/debt that had preciously enabled them to afford the goods and services of the real economy.

**Keywords** Crisis of overproduction • Housing bubble • Underwater mortgages

Notwithstanding the fact that the *dialectical contradiction* at the heart of capitalism, resulting as it does in crises of overproduction, supposedly inevitably portends its ultimate collapse, capitalism both survives and apparently thrives. Thus despite the fact that, for instance, median



S. Glynn, *The Economic Logic of Late Capitalism and the Inevitable Triumph of Socialism*,
https://doi.org/10.1007/978-3-030-52667-2_9

*individual* income in the US (responding to downward pressure on wages resulting from economic competition) actually fell significantly, from around $46,000 to about $34,000 per annum (in inflation adjusted dollars) in the 25 years between 1982 and the onset of the Great Recession in 2007, the US economy grew significantly (GDP doubling from around $7 Trillion per annum in 1980 to around $14 Trillion per annum in that period, and was, prior to the coronavirus pandemic, standing at around $22 Trillion) which would seem to provide *empirical* refutation of Marx's claim, and the *theoretical* analysis upon which it was based. Nor can the *increase* in GDP over this period be accounted for by increased demand emanating from increased workforce participation, for this merely enabled the *maintenance* of median annual *household* income at around $54,000. Moreover, although it is therefore clear from these figures that the benefits of this increase in production must have gone as profits to capital or capitalists, who profited both from the decrease in production costs or wages and from lending to the therefore increasingly impercunious workers, and while such profits generated a certain increase in demand for high-end luxury goods (reflected, for instance, in the rapid increase in prices in the high-end art market, to give but one example) much was also saved (as evidenced by the rapid accumulation of wealth over that period, to the point where the top 1% of US Citizens now own much more wealth than the bottom 90% combined) and much of this surplus accumulation was reinvested (as evidenced by the 18 fold increase, from 776 to 14,164, in the Dow Jones Index over this same 25 year period). Furthermore, much of that which wasn't simply reinvested in the US economy went to foreign economies, where production costs were, in large part due to even lower wage levels, less. All of which would seem to portend not only *depressed* domestic demand, but, due to such lower wages, depressed *foreign* demand *relative to production*! And so far from US export earnings being able to account for the robust US consumer demand exhibited across the economic spectrum during this period, the US has long imported more than it has exported, as the growing national debt attests; a circumstance that simultaneously *added to the supply* of goods (and, to a lesser extent, outsourced services) *and*, as money to pay for these imports flowed out, *reduced domestic demand* for domestically produced, and indeed all, goods and services. How then, without either a substantial increase in aggregated national wages, or a reduction in prices which would clearly have had a negative effect on GDP, was the US economy able to avoid a crisis of overproduction?

The answer is, of course, in a word, *credit*. While given that their homes are the major, not to say quite literally concrete (or bricks and mortar) asset of the general public, it was mortgages that initially became the major vehicle for the extension of this necessary credit. The increased availability and accessibility of mortgages fueling a rise in property prices, which not only underwrote secondary mortgages or home equity loans that boosted consumer spending, but which, by ensuring that in the event of the borrower's default the lenders were left with an appreciating asset (the home) that could therefore be sold at a profit, additionally meant that lenders had no reason either to insist upon large up front deposits as insurance against default, or to be concerned more generally about the credit worthiness or ability of would-be mortgagees to service their mortgage debt. Rather, on the contrary, they had every reason to promote subprime[1] loans and other forms of predatory lending, in the hope of such default. *A strategy that enabled the money lenders or capitalists to suck up a vast proportion of the accumulated assets of middle-class home owners.* While such easy lending, by increasing demand for properties, thereby, to complete the circle, produced the very increase in property values which literally underwrote or insured the lending which gave rise to it. A ***self-generating*** "housing bubble," sustained by *the extension of mortgages to the ever less qualified, and eventually entirely unqualified, borrowers.* And as if this were not sufficient cause for concern, the housing boom attracted financial speculators into the market, who saw such rapidly appreciating property not as residences (or *real* assets) *per se*, but as investment opportunities (or *financial* assets). Investors who, in entering the market in large numbers, and thus constituting a secondary market, drove demand, and therefore prices, up still further, thus producing a second, *speculatively driven*, inflationary bubble, so significant that it continued to drive up residential prices despite the fact that speculators also invested in new construction, and thus supplied more houses to the market. An increase in home equity that encouraged further borrowing, in the form of home equity loans, or second mortgages, taken out by home owners, anxious to leverage, and thus benefit from, the increasing value of their residential properties or asset.

Thus the increasing availability of credit, in providing further equity to invest in housing, was thereby *both cause and consequence* of the housing boom, which in addition to thereby stimulating demand for the products of, and thereby providing opportunities to invest in, associated industries, such as the residential insurance market and other real estate servicing industries, and household goods, and so on, also, in affording home equity

[1] See Chapter 1, footnote 1.

loans and the like, underwrote demand across the whole economy, resulting in what then US Treasury Secretary Alan Greenspan famously termed "irrational exuberance." Irrational even to the extent that such an expanding economy encouraged even those who had no real estate holdings, or indeed not much equity of any description, to be optimistic about their future earning capacity, and consequently more than willing to borrow extensively on their credit cards; US credit card debt standing at around $1.3 Trillion. While students and their parents, who were for the same reason optimistic concerning future employment opportunities and earning capacity, happily took on student loan debt—which at around $1.5 Trillion exceeded even credit card debt—so that *they* could assume the financial burden of job training in any and all of the skills which they assumed *employers* would continue to require in order to profit from.[2]

Indeed the provision of such credit boosted demand for goods and services, even as wages, and therefore production costs, declined, not only staving off a crisis of overproduction, but substantially boosting the profits of the capitalist investors in the *real* economy which provided goods and non-financial services. And additionally low wages also profited the capitalist investors in the *financial* economy, for they ensured buoyant demand for credit, thereby boosting the profits derivable by those in a position to provide it via the aforementioned home equity loans, credit cards, student loans and other instruments! Indeed, so successful was this strategy that while between 1982 and 2007, as we have noted, the (inflation adjusted) median wage fell by around 30% while Gross Domestic Product increased by 100%, the financial sector's corporate profits, rose from around 15% of GDP in 1985 to about 40% by 2008.[3] To reiterate, *the reduction in wages not only reduced production*

[2] Quite clearly a good argument can be made to the effect that the cost of job training, at least for jobs in the private sector, should fall, as indeed it did in the apprenticeship system, upon employers, and thus ultimately upon the investor classes, who will profit from their skilled workforce. In which case it is these employers and investors who should either provide training directly, or indirectly by financing, via their taxes, all public education except that of the estimated proportion of the student population that will enter public service, whose education should be financed by taxes levied upon the general population who will benefit from their service. In fact, government financing of higher education, through taxes levied upon both corporate profits and individual income, was practiced throughout much of Europe at least after WWII, until comparatively recently, where increasing capture of the political process by the wealthy investor class, together with international competition (of which more later) is increasingly resulting in its being abandoned even there.

[3] See referenced article in Chapter 6, footnote 1.

*costs, enabling the rich to get richer due to the increased profitability of the real economy, but also increased the demand of the low waged for credit, consequently enabling the rich, who were in a position to supply it, to profit enormously from the financial economy also. A two pronged strategy of squeezing the poor from both ends*—accounting for an estimated four-fold increase in wealth of the top 1% during that time—which not only enabled the rich to get richer *at the expense of the poor*, but largely to get richer ***to the extent to which*** *the poor got poorer*!

All went swingingly, for the rich at least, until the capacity of speculators to raise more financing from already hugely overleveraged[4] collateral, compounded with the realization that the accumulating value of the housing stock *ultimately* depended upon the ability of those whose median wage had declined—and who consequently were ever more burdened by the debt accumulating on the credit upon which they were increasingly forced to rely—to be able to purchase such housing at the then prevailing, speculatively *inflated*, prices, lead to concern among speculators about the real, underlying, value of both the *concrete* domestic real estate assets, and *financially securitized* (real estate backed or collateralized) *debt obligations*, they were holding. This resulted first in a leveling off of prices, and then to an accelerating drop, followed by a precipitous fall, as *speculative investors* rushing to offload their "assets" before the market went any lower, glutted it with both *concrete housing and real estate securities* (i.e. the securitized mortgage debt that had paid for the housing) offered at ever lower prices. And as if this self-reinforcing downward spiral and concomitant bursting of the speculative bubble were not bad enough, the fall in residential real estate values not only also left a large number of *actual residents* who had bought their housing relatively lately, with outstanding mortgage *principle* which was very much greater than the falling market value of their houses—which is to say with negative equity or "underwater" mortgages—but in addition, similarly left those earlier entrants who had subsequently taken out home equity loans and the like, with negative equity. A circumstance leading many to simply "walk away" from their debt, which resulted in an increasing rate of mortgage defaults and foreclosures, and *a further glut in housing and real estate securities*, which put more downward pressure on housing prices and the value of real estate securities, resulting in more and more people having negative equity or debt, and so on and on, just as financial institutions had more and more

[4] For an account of leveraging see Chapter 1, footnote 2.

increasingly valueless real estate collateralized securities or financial "assets."

With many current and former mortgage borrowers, and those who had taken out second mortgages or home equity loans and so on having, quite literally, negative equity, or less than nothing to spend on goods and services, there was, of course, a dramatically reduced demand in the rest of the economy. This meant that many of those who had taken out mortgages, home equity, credit card and student loans on the basis of their reasonable anticipation of continued employment, now faced unemployment, or at least reduced hours, and were consequently unable to continue to pay even the interest on them, which resulted in yet more foreclosures, bad credit ratings, and overall debt, both for them and for financial institutions; graduating students being particularly hard hit, as the hoped for employment that they had supposed would enable them to pay back their student loans, dried up.

CHAPTER 10

# Overleveraging, the Cascading Debt Crisis, and the Necessary Inadequacy of Increased Regulation in the Face of the Inevitable Crisis of Overproduction

**Abstract** Mortgage companies sold on the mortgages or debt obligations they held, to other financial institutions, which provided them with more money to finance further mortgages which could be likewise securitized, and so on. A *leveraging* which when housing prices collapsed left these financial institutions with inadequate collateral to cover their extensively overleveraged loans, resulting in a cascading debt crisis and implosion of financial markets. This left them, and those who had extended credit via credit cards and student loans and so on, unable to extend further credit when it was most needed by indebted borrowers to meet basic living costs, which resulted in a general economic depression and recession. A recession resulting from the overextension of credit which, as previously noted, was invoked by a crisis of overproduction *ultimately* rooted in an intranscendable contradiction at the heart of capitalism.

**Keywords** Crisis of overproduction • Leveraging • Cascading debt crisis • Immediate and ultimate cause • Capitalist contradiction

It would, I believe, be wrong to assume that it was merely due to an oversight, or perhaps we should better say lack thereof, that the overextension of credit and excessive leveraging, which were the immediate, if not the ultimate, cause of the Great Recession came about. For the urgency with which, in late 2005, just ahead of the meltdown, the law regulating



S. Glynn, *The Economic Logic of Late Capitalism and the Inevitable Triumph of Socialism*,
https://doi.org/10.1007/978-3-030-52667-2_10

personal bankruptcy was changed[1] so as to impose greater financial obligations on the defaulting borrower before she/he could emerge from bankruptcy, would seem to suggest otherwise. Nevertheless, despite such defensive maneuvers, the dramatic fall in domestic real estate values left mortgage companies, for whom the properties on which they had extended mortgages acted as collateral that supposedly underwrote the risk of default, with negative equity also, as it did those financial institutions which had bought the securitized derivatives, which is to say the debt obligations, derived from such mortgages. And the process of leveraging, by which the money from selling such securities had been used to finance further mortgages, from which further debt obligations were derived and securitized, to be sold on (etc.) resulted in a cascading debt crisis.[2] With inadequate real estate collateral to cover their mortgage and securities investments, these financial institutions and markets imploded; those financial institutions which had extended consumer credit on credit cards, student loans and by other means, facing similar difficulties. This then left them unable to extend credit precisely at a time when it was most needed by increasingly indebted borrowers in order to meet their living costs; which in turn left companies in the real economy with excessive inventories of goods, and excess service generating capacity, even as it put ever greater downward pressure on retail prices, thus constituting a crisis of overproduction and a massive recession, complete with mounting unemployment.

Perhaps unsurprisingly, capitalist apologists, ever concerned with damage control, rushed to blame it all, if not entirely on the "irrational exuberance" of individuals, then, upon the most obvious, and, more importantly, remediable, flaws in the market finance system. First up for criticism was the extension of mortgages to many admittedly unqualified mortgage borrowers, and the closely associated "predatory lending," underwritten by the very buoyancy of the housing market that such activity had itself largely produced. Next up for criticism was the fraudulent

[1] Whereas under "Chapter 7" bankruptcy, having had their personal assets liquidated in favor of their creditors, debtors were able to have their remaining debts canceled, the new law forced more people into "Chapter 11," by which individuals could be forced into a further five-year repayment plan before being allowed to emerge from bankruptcy. The concern here NOT being whether such requirements are reasonable or not, but whether this tightening of the law indicates, as I believe it does, a prescience which undermines the widely broadcast claim that "no one understood what was happening."

[2] For an account of leveraging, see Chapter 1, footnote 2.

"Triple A" ratings given, by rating agencies such as Arthur Anderson, to inadequately collateralized securitized debt obligations and their derivatives, and the massive "overleveraging" that it helped facilitate. Thus it is suggested by these capitalist apologists that rigorous enforcement of adequate qualification criteria for mortgagees and others to whom credit is extended, together with the limiting of overleveraging and high-risk speculation in securitized debt obligations, and so on, all of which could be achieved by responsible and effective financial regulation—although of course completely at odds with the "free market" to which capitalists are so devoted, until, of course, it is not in their interests to be so—would go a long way toward ensuring that nothing like the Great Recession would be "allowed" to happen again. Indeed consequently some even went so far as to countenance, at least publically, such an affront to the "free market," as the reinstatement of something like the Glass/Steagall Act,[3] in order to limit the potentially adverse effects of "casino" capitalism as they now referred to overly speculative finance capitalism in a disingenuous attempt to suggest that they should not only be distinguished from, but, further, regarded as dissociated from, it!

Now, in light of the undeniable fact that lax credit restrictions, aided by overleveraging and other forms of excessive financial speculation facilitated, at least in part, by speculators access to commercial bank deposits, was the *immediate* cause of the crash, it might seem reasonable to accept this view that all that was really required to avert future crashes was little more than such regulatory tinkering. However what this fails to recognize is that, although admittedly grossly inadequate regulation certainly exacerbated the problem, as close attention to the preceding analysis reveals, *the (over)extension of ultimately unserviceable debt obligations or credit is/was in fact a necessary precondition of putting of, or deferring, an inevitable crisis of overproduction. A crisis of overproduction, brought about by a combination of increased production and falling wages, which is the unavoidable or*

[3] This regulation, introduced in 1933 in the wake of the Wall Street Crash of 1929, and the ensuing Great Depression, limited the capacity of commercial banks to deal and invest in financial securities, and thus investment banking from gambling with the financial capital derived from commercial bank depositors. However increasingly lax interpretations, by federal bank regulators, of the restrictions imposed by this act, rendered it increasingly impotent until it was eventually repealed in 1999. While even though the Dodd-Frank Act passed under the Obama administration, had already been considerably weakened by finance industry lobbying, the Trump administration wasted no time in attempting to roll back financial regulation still further. (See Chapter 2, footnote 4).

*inevitable consequence of free market competition, and the efficiency that survival in such a market demands. Inevitable, because of course*—unless debt is to be forgiven, which may save "the capitalist system" only by completely transforming it, albeit perhaps temporally, into a form of socialism—*borrowed money has to be repaid; the cost of servicing debt resulting in a reduction of disposable income, and therefore ultimately exacerbating the very problem that the extension of credit was initiated to solve.*[4]

Thus *the underlying contradiction at the heart of laissez-faire capitalism will inevitably result, if not in its immediately demise, then, as Marx predicted, in ever more frequent and severe cyclical fluctuations as deflation, stemming from the crisis of overproduction, is followed by the re-inflation resulting from the credit driven attempt to stimulate demand.* The downside or deflationary component of such fluctuations giving rise to ever more frequent and severe bankruptcies of companies, corporations, people, and governments, as the reduction in wages required to remain competitive in face of the falling prices resulting from increased competition driven productivity or efficiency serves to increasingly or further suppress aggregate demand relative to output. A reduction in aggregate demand which in further reducing prices and profits, necessitates further reductions in wages/employment, and thus taxable revenues, and so on and on; a "race to the bottom," which will, sooner or later, inevitably end in the demise of capitalism!

[4] Indeed, depending on the interest rate, a 30-year fixed rate domestic mortgage not untypically ends up costing the borrower around 250% of the initial loan. And although the final value of the residence at the time the mortgage is paid off may have appreciated by that much or more, it must of course be remembered that this has to be discounted to reflect inflation, and the concomitant decrease in the value of money, over the repayment period. And even if the borrower invests in property which appreciates sufficiently that she/he emerges with an asset worth more, even when adjusted for inflation, than the mortgage payments she/he made, such appreciation is, of course, profit rather than wages. Profit which is itself *ultimately* dependent, in the long run, not upon speculative bubbles fueled by eventually demand sapping credit but, upon the maintenance of a robust demand for housing from potential residents, and thus upon their healthy income levels. Healthy income levels which will succumb in the long run to the pressures of free market competition!

CHAPTER 11

# The Counter Narrative of the Long-Term Upward Trajectory of Capitalism, and Its Costs Critically Explicated: From Colonialism to Economic Neo-Colonialization

**Abstract** While crises of overproduction may indeed be periodic, quasi-Malthusian, cyclical fluctuations, nevertheless capitalism's long-term trajectory has been upward. This was previously explained by colonialization. The exploiting of cheap foreign resources or/and labor, enabling capitalists to remain competitively productive or efficient even while keeping the wages of their consequently embourgeoised domestic workforce sufficiently high to ensure buoyant demand. A function later fulfilled by economic neo-colonialization. Yet even when free market competition among *developed* nations for the *underdeveloped* nations' resource and/or labor may drive the costs thereof sufficiently high to enable previously *underdeveloped* supplier nations to accrue enough capital to begin to aspire to the status of *developing* nations, competition between them will ultimately put downward pressure on resource and labor costs, and environmental and safety standards.

**Keywords** Colonialization • Economic neo-colonialization • Embourgeoised • Environmental and safety standards

Although all of the preceding analysis may seem to explain the series of capitalist crises—ranging, one may argue, from the downside of the cyclical fluctuations identified almost 200 years ago by Malthus to the Great Depression of the 1930s, up to the Great Recession of 2008 and



S. Glynn, *The Economic Logic of Late Capitalism and the Inevitable Triumph of Socialism*,
https://doi.org/10.1007/978-3-030-52667-2_11

on—marked by falling profits, wages, and employment, nevertheless optimists point out that such downturns are cyclical. While although upside recovery, being largely credit fueled will, for reasons already analyzed in considerable detail, inevitably be followed by recessions, nevertheless *the long-term overarching trajectory of capitalism has been a demonstrable and massive increase in profits, and a substantial increase in wages, in light of which such cyclical fluctuations appear as temporary "noise."* And that so far from necessarily being ever more frequent and severe, such deviations from the normal upward trajectory have, at times, gone through periods of diminishing magnitude and frequency.

And yet, such *empirical* observation notwithstanding, the *logic* of Marx's argument remains unassailable. An apparent contradiction, which Lenin—who was not unsurprisingly concerned to understand how, despite Marx's analysis, Britain, France, Holland, Belgium, Spain, Portugal, and other Western European capitalist nations had survived and even increasingly prospered—explained in a single word: *colonialization*. Moreover it should be observed that just as it was military and transport technology that largely enabled colonialization, so too, notwithstanding the claims of capitalist apologists to the contrary, *it was, of course, also precisely technological innovation more generally, as opposed to capitalism per se, which was responsible for the aforementioned upward trajectory of so many of the world's economies.*

As Lenin saw then, colonialization facilitated an exploitative dominance of other nations or economies not entirely dissimilar to the exploitative dominance which the capitalist classes, by virtue of their monopolization of the technologies of production, asserted at a national level over the proletariat within their own nations or economies. A domination which enabled the *colonizing* nations to monopolize the utilization or consumption of the labor and resources of the *colonized* nations at low enough costs that, even while keeping the wages of their (the colonizer's) own workforce high enough to maintain buoyant domestic demand, they could keep overall production costs low enough to remain competitive and profitable. A strategy which thereby clearly forestalled any supposedly otherwise pending crisis of overproduction. Although, predicated as it was upon the colonization and *enforced* exploitation of the workforce and resources of the colonized, *the surviving capitalism was no more of the laissez-faire or free-market variety than were the domestic workforce of the colonizing nations*—who as Lenin pointed out, were embourgeoised by this exploitation of the colonized—*thoroughgoing members of the proletariat* properly so called.[1]

More recently, of course, colonization has tended to evolve into more *indirect military*, and/or *economic, neo-colonialization*, by which nations such as the US, Great Britain and France, for example, supply advanced military hardware and other technologies to prop up, and even help establish, political power elites in other nations[2] prepared to collude with them in extracting cheap resources or/and utilizing cheap, or low paid, labor, and/or by which, alternatively, they (the neo-colonializers) invest directly or—by extending credit—indirectly, in developing and undeveloped economies. A strategy which, by increasingly bringing these nations into the capitalist-dominated economic marketplace, is touted as a way of lifting these economies, and those who work for them, out of poverty. A claim made all the more plausible by the fact that, *at least in theory*, international competition between developed economies for the labor and resources of underdeveloped economies, in putting upward pressure on the underdeveloped economies' wages and resource prices, increasingly turn these undeveloped and developing economies from being suppliers of resources, goods and services, into emerging markets or consumers thereof. A turn of events which in addition to thereby *seemingly* vanquishing the previously analyzed, and otherwise clearly major, *ontological* threat to capitalism's *long-term* survival posed by crises of overproduction, to the contrary makes it possible, in the longer term, for the developing nations to accumulate sufficient capital from both rising wages and resource prices, that, when invested in (productive) technology, should allow them to contest any residual exploitation, albeit often asymmetrically.[3] An exporting of capitalist grounded

[1] That is to say that the ability of the capitalist enterprises to remain competitive even while paying relatively robust wages to their domestic "proletariat," being dependent upon the exploitation of cheap colonial resources and labor, therefore entails the domestic workforce being, though not direct recipients, nevertheless beneficiaries, of the *profits* derived from such exploitation, therefore diminishing their purely proletarian status.

[2] For instance the overthrow of the democratically elected Mohammad Mosaddegh by the US backed, so-called, Shah of Iran (Mohammad Pahlavi), and of democratically elected Salvador Allende of Chile by the fascist military dictatorship of Augusto Pinochet, the support of the regime of Hosni Mubarak, and subsequently of the military dictatorship of Abdel el-Sisi, who overthrew the democratically elected Muslim Brotherhood in Egypt, not to mention the US's previous support for any number of other dictatorships in South and Central America, and continuing support for similarly ones in the Middle East and Africa.

[3] Thus the advent and development of the roadside bomb, not to mention the possibility of making a nuclear bomb with 5 of the several hundred Kilograms of Plutonium per year

prosperity which is heralded by capitalists as "a rising tide that lifts all boats."

Rosy as this picture may appear however, there are, in fact, many *de facto* impediments to such developments. While, more tellingly, even if and when these *de facto* impediments can be overcome, the economic logic of *laissez-faire* or free-market capitalist competition will nevertheless, *a priori* or inevitably, result in a "race to the bottom."

Thus beginning with the *de facto* impediments, given that, as noted, many of the political and economic power elites in much of the underdeveloped or neo-colonialized world are, if not directly brought to power, then indirectly supported and maintained in power, by the military technology, training, and other assistance they receive from the more developed neo-colonizing nations, they will either be in no position to entertain potential alternative competitors for their labor and resources, or at the very least, reluctant to do so, for fear of their patrons replacing them with more compliant leadership.[4] A circumstance which pressures leaders of the undeveloped and underdeveloped economies to collaborate with their neo-colonizing patrons both in suppressing demands made by the former's workforce for increased wages and benefits, and in ensuring that resource prices remain relatively low, all to the advantage of the developed economies. Whatever financial benefits the undeveloped or relatively underdeveloped economies manage to accrue from such asymmetric arrangements tending to flow disproportionately to their political elites. Elites which, insofar as they continue to derive such benefits from the

produced by even a single 1000 Megawatt nuclear reactor—a bomb which, even without a detonator could nevertheless destroy a few blocks of, say New York, and make the whole city uninhabitable for approximately 250,000 years (i.e. approximately 10 time the Half Life of Plutonium)—enables those with even primitive technologies of their own to contest, albeit asymmetrically, military domination by those with more advanced weapons technologies, just as low wages and health and safety standards, and laxer environmental standards and labor laws, as well, perhaps, as easier access to resources, similarly makes it possible for those with less productive or efficient technologies to contest the economic domination of those with more productive or efficient technologies.

[4] Thus the US Joint Combined Exchange Program (JCEP) has programs in 110 countries where they train foreign militaries in advanced sniper, close combat, urban military and other foreign defense and domestic security operations, and like the former School of the Americas, and Western Hemisphere Institute for Security Operations which succeeded it, has, in conjunction with US Special Forces, often supported foreign regimes which cooperate in the co-option of their economies by US economic interests, and been instrumental in overthrowing those that opposed such US hegemony.

prevailing state of affairs, have little incentive to invest this income—preferring instead to spend it on their own, often unimaginably conspicuous, consumption—unless, of course, they fear for their economic and/or political futures. In which case, with little incentive to invest in their own, potentially unstable, economies, *which investment would, in any event, likely give rise to an increasingly powerful middle class who might challenge their authority*, they overwhelmingly prefer to invest in established foreign economies.

Turning now from these *de facto* impediments to those resulting, *a priori*, from the economic logic of *laissez-faire* or free-market capitalist competition. Even when the underdeveloped economies and their leadership are not only free, but willing and able, in an attempt to improve the economic prosperity of their general population, to seek out alternative utilizers or consumers of their labor and resources from among the developed economies—*developed economies* which might thus be forced to compete with each other for such labor and resources, thereby potentially raising the revenues to the developing economies—nevertheless these *emerging* or *developing economies*, as participants in a competitive, even if not entirely free, market, must in turn, of course, compete with one another in doing so. A circumstance that, as when they were *intentionally* serving the interests of those in the developed economies of the neo-colonialists, also results in downward pressure on wages, benefits, and resource prices, as well as further cost reduction by the lowering of safety, health, and environmental standards, as unequivocally illustrated by the explosion of Union Carbide's production facility in Bhopal, India, and the collapse of the Rana Plaza garment factory in Bangladesh[5] to give but two of many, many, examples.

[5] The Bhopal explosion immediately resulted in 3787 deaths (considerably more than 9/11) and 3900 severe permanent injuries, followed by 8000 more deaths within two weeks, and in excess of a *further* 8000 gas-related deaths thereafter, while the collapse of the Rana Plaza facility, where major international corporations were producing clothes for export to the advanced economies, resulted in 1134 deaths and approximately 2500 injuries. Foreign events not entirely unlike domestic, similarly capitalist profit driven, events, such as the collapse of The Upper Big Branch mine in West Virginia (which as an extraction operation of domestic resources could not be outsourced)—resulting from a "conspiracy to willfully violate safety standards" (the mine received 2 safety citations the day before the explosion, 600 in the preceding 18 months, and 1342 in the preceding five years)—in which 29 miners died. An accident for which, perhaps unsurprisingly given already explicated corporate capture of the political process, and consequent influence over both law, and, more indirectly, judicial appointments, Massy Energy's CEO Don Blankenship received nothing more than a 1-year prison sentence!

CHAPTER 12

# The Transnational Capitalist Pyramid of Production or Supposed "Rising Tide That Lifts all Boats," Revealed, as an Inevitably Failing Ponzi Scheme

**Abstract** Despite engagement of the *developed* economies with the less developed appearing to be a win/win "rising tide (of capitalism) which lifts all boats," competition *between developing* economies, and with *potential* competitors further down the *pyramid of production*, puts downward pressure on *wages* and *resource* prices. And so too with *developed* economies, which, in addition to peer group competition, will experience competition from *developing* economies, as attested to by stagnating and even decreasing wages resulting from outsourcing for instance. This results in a lose/lose "race to the bottom" as economies at every level try to become more competitive by cutting cost, and therefore wages and, concomitantly, demand, both precipitating and exacerbating crises of overproduction and the collapse of what thus stands revealed as the "*Ponzi Scheme*" or *pyramid* of exploitative *laissez-faire* capitalism.

**Keywords** Win/win • Lose/lose • Rising tide • Race to the bottom • Creative destruction

The fact that it is only by accepting low wages and benefits, and health, safety, and environmental standards, that the *developing* economies remain competitive (albeit asymmetrically) with technologically more advanced



S. Glynn, *The Economic Logic of Late Capitalism and the Inevitable Triumph of Socialism*,
https://doi.org/10.1007/978-3-030-52667-2_12

and therefore potentially more efficient or productive economies, would seem to be indicative of the ineluctably exploitative nature of capitalist competition. And yet, on the other hand, the willingness of those at the bottom of the pyramid of production to nevertheless continue to produce basic commodities under such conditions may be seen as a reflection of their recognition and acceptance of what is often, quite literally, a life-saving option. Furthermore it is to be acknowledged that previously undeveloped, and indeed developing, economies have, in part as a consequence of international trade with the developed economies, on occasion developed sufficiently to produce at least some of the same goods as the developed economies produce. Thus following WWII Germany and Japan were able, by virtue of subsequent government planning of educational systems designed to produce both exceptional technical researchers and a workforce of highly skilled engineers, technicians, designers, managers, and so on, and, *with the help of Marshall Aid* and the like, to innovate, deploy, and operate a range of advanced technologies which—as the success of, for example, Mercedes, Audi, Porsche, Volkswagen, Honda, and Toyota demonstrate—enable them to produce automobiles, together, of course, with other advanced technological products of a ***quality***, and even of a ***sort or type***, with which the developed economies of the Allies found, and continue to find, it increasingly difficult to compete. While similar, South-Korea, Brazil, India, and other, initially less technologically competent, economies currently compete in certain, although typically more limited, areas also.

In light of this, it would *seem* that free-market capitalist competition fosters technological innovation, and thus brings out the best in all, as developing economies attempt to catch up, and developed economies continue to innovate in order to stay ahead. A fostering of competitively driven technological innovation that results in increasing demand from both the *developed* and *developing* economies for the basic resources and commodities of the *undeveloped* economies, thereby enabling them too to escape poverty. While such competition also motivates the developing economies to follow the developed economies up the value-added curve—from the production of items such as textiles and basic clothing, houseware and ceramics, and so on, to the production of commodities such as steel and "white goods," such as domestic washing machines and refrigerators, as well as televisions, automobiles, and eventually computers, aircraft, and the like—thereby enabling the developed economies to concentrate on the production of ever more advanced technologies. And although the developing economies *may generally* find that they are unable to catch up with the developed economies, just as the undeveloped economies *may generally* find that they cannot catch up with the developing economies, demand from the developed economies for the products of the developing economies, together with the fact that workers in the developing economies, often finding themselves unable to purchase many of the products of the developed economies, are *willing* to purchase their own products, will enable both to prosper. This then, together with increasing demand for basic resources and commodities supplied by the underdeveloped economies to support all this, will surely mean that they too will prosper. Thus exploitative as current arrangements surely are—annual world GDP standing, prior to the coronavirus pandemic, at around $88 trillion, divided by a planetary population of around 7.8 billion people, would result in an *average* income of over $11,000 per head ($44,000 for a family of 4), while in fact approaching 2 billion, or more than 1 in 4 of the planetary population live on under $2 a day[1]—nevertheless the wages and other benefits that one might reasonably expect to flow as a consequence of the increase in demand emanating from general economic growth, will surely lift ever more out of abject poverty. Capitalist competition, which *appears* to be a zero-sum win/lose game[2] (where some win at the expense of others who lose the competition), thereby *ostensibly* being thus converted into a win/win situation as *laissez-faire* or free-market competition *seemingly* facilitates "a rising tide which lifts all boats."

Unfortunately however, things are not quite what they may seem. Thus beginning with Germany and Japan, let it not be forgotten that pre-war both were already highly technically competent. While even more significantly, post-war both economies, so far from being *laissez-faire* or free market, benefited enormously from international subsidies, extensive government intervention, and restrictive trade agreements, just as South-Korea, Brazil, India, and others have benefited from similarly, although admittedly perhaps less extensive, programs. And as for the "rising tide" win/win argument, notwithstanding the demand emanating from the more developed economies for the basic products of the developing economies and resources of the undeveloped economies, which they and their

[1] Nor can it be argued, as some have tried, that $2 in a third world country purchase more than in the US as the purchasing power of the third world "wretched of the earth" is computed in terms of the purchasing power of $'s in the US!

[2] See Chapter 1, footnote 4.

workers rely upon to fuel their advancement and growth, nevertheless, in a free market, developing and underdeveloped economies will, as just now noted, each be in competition with their peer economies, thus putting downward pressure on wages, resource prices, and other elements beneficial to the less developed economies, that might otherwise be expected to flow from general economic growth and demand. While even if, notwithstanding such competitive downward pressure on wages and other potentially demand stimulating benefits, some sectors of the less developed economies nevertheless manage to emerge as markets for the developed economies' products, this will in no way enable the developed economies, and indeed the pyramid of production dependent upon their demand, to avoid a crisis of overproduction. For to the extent that such *emerging markets* are fueled by the money the more developed economies pay for their (the less developed economies') products and resources, this reduces the more developed economies' capacity to purchase the products that *they* (the developed economies) themselves, as well as any *other* economies dependent upon their demand, produce. Any increase in demand from less developed economies' emerging markets clearly being derived at the expense of decreasing demand from the more developed economies.[3] A problem greatly exacerbated by the fact that only if the *cost* of the less developed economies' resources and products—and consequently, other things being equal, the demand emerging from these less developed economies—is *less* than they would be if the developed economies produced them themselves, will the latter purchase such products from the former in the first place.

And just as competition from peer economies, and from those, often with more developed economies and technologies, further *up* the pyramid of production, puts downward pressure on the wages, benefits, and other potential purchasing power of those further *down*, so competition from peer economies, and those further *down*, puts downward pressure upon the wages, benefits, and other potential purchasing power of those further *up*. Thus the emergence of competition, initially from the West German

[3] Were it not for the fact that this exacerbates the crisis of overproduction, this downward redistribution of purchasing power would lift the less well-off economies, which even if achieved, as we shall now see, at a cost to the more well-off economies, would—in light of the diminishing marginal utility of wealth (e.g., the increased benefit or utility to be derived from say an extra $5 by a rich person being less than that derived by someone living on less than $2 a day)—from a Utilitarian perspective (see Chapter 8, footnote 1) tend to be desirable.

and Japanese automotive industries, not to mention the South Korean Hyundai-Kia group, and subsequently from Jaguar and Range Rover—acquired by India's TATA motors from Ford at knock down prices as a consequence of falling demand resulting from such competition and the Great Recession—forced Chrysler and General Motors into Chapter 11 bankruptcy in 2009.

Clearly then, so far from "lifting all boats" as capitalism's apologists claim, as we previously saw with regard to less developed economies, so too with developed economies, the rising tide of *capitalist competition* results in the less seaworthy or competitive sectors of even the more advanced economies becoming "underwater wrecks." In light of which, these apologists immediately change "tack," celebrating such wreckage as the "flotsam" and "jetsam" of Schumpeter's "creative destruction."[4] That is to say that they then insist, with some justification, that such bankruptcies are, in fact, free-market capitalist competition operating as it supposedly should, to ensure that only the fittest survive; those who are uncompetitive being forced to *technologically innovate*[5] *and/or cut wages, and thus reduce production costs*, which is to say to become more *efficient*, and thus competitive or fit enough to survive.

Not that this has precluded capitalist corporations, for all their celebration of the evolutionary benefits supposedly flowing from the "natural" selection of the fittest and concomitant destruction of the less fit by the competitive free market, from accepting government intervention to support the less fit when it suits them. However, having emerged from Chapter 11 Bankruptcy thanks to *socialist* intervention in the form of government orchestrated, taxpayer-funded, "bailouts"[6]—which effectively

[4] See Schumpeter, J. (1942) 1994. *Capitalism, Socialism and Democracy*. London: Routledge: p. 139. Note this was derived from Marx's notion of the accumulation and annihilation of capital, first outlined in *The Communist Manifesto*, and later refined in the *Grundrisse* and *Das Kapital*.

[5] Technology taken here, as before, to refer not only to machinery but productive systems, and technological innovation therefore being taken to include radical restructuring thereof.

[6] Socialist, of course, by virtue *both* of the fact that this intervention prioritized social goals, such as jobs and employment, above the economic logic of profit-driven capitalist competition, and because, as taxpayer-funded, this intervention was socially financed. Although having assumed, on behalf of the taxpayers, the downside risk/cost, as soon as these companies again turned a profit the bought and paid for politicians, knowing who they really work for, immediately relinquished ownership on behalf of the general public in favor of private investors so that they, rather than the general public, could derive these upside profits.

nationalized them, and gave them sufficient capital to develop new, more attractive, product—GM and Chrysler wasted no time in proclaiming that the competitive ethos of the free market left them with no alternative other than to cut benefits and savagely slash wages—although tellingly not to instead accept decreased profits—and outsource supply chains to even more poorly paid workers in less developed economies, as the price of their continued survival! A reduction in wages and other benefits which, contra Henry Ford's philosophy of paying his workers well enough for them to be able to afford his automobiles, made it more difficult for workers to afford the automobiles they produced. Similarly, competitively driven downward pressure on wages and benefits across the entire economy resulted in a reduction in aggregate demand, which although compensated for to a limited degree by a variety of government demand side incentives or stimuli, nevertheless has tellingly led, if not to the bankruptcies of many other companies, to their very slow rate of recovery.

Thus as we can now perhaps see, the rise of the less developed economies puts downward pressure on the wages, benefits, and concomitant demand of workers in the more developed economies, while insofar as the less developed economies are themselves in a transparent, competitive, free market, they have to engage in cost cutting competition with their peers as well as with those further down the pyramid of production who are able to compete, all of which puts downward pressure on their wages, benefits, and demand also. Consequently, so far from capitalist competition in such a market resulting in a win/win "rising tide that lifts all boats," or even a zero-sum game in which the fittest win or survive at the expense of the less fit, who lose or sink, absent government intervention it in fact results in a lose/lose "race to the bottom," which threatens to sink all boats, whether national or international. It being, of course, just such free-market competition from emerging economies which, contributing to the previously mentioned downward pressure on US wages—to the extent that the median wage decreased from $46,000 in 1982 to $34,000 (in constant, inflation adjusted dollars) in 2007—as it did, exacerbated the inevitable crisis of overproduction and accompanying loss of *profits and* jobs or *wages*, that would, in any case, eventually have resulted from peer competition. A downward pressure which, so long as the aforementioned characteristics of the globalized free market remain operative, can never be subject to long-term abatement. And if the concomitant increasing loss of the *privilege* of the embourgeoised proletariat or workers in the economically developed nations, derived at the expense of the economic exploitation of others—a loss of privilege often misunderstood by those who previously benefited from it as increased *oppression*—does not consequently lead to an economic reordering, then it will, of course, result in the collapse of what now stands revealed as the "*Ponzi Scheme*" or *pyramid* of exploitative *laissez-faire* capitalism.

CHAPTER 13

# Overt Abandonment of the Free Market: Government Geostrategic (Military) and Economic, International and National Intervention

**Abstract** Given the crises of overproduction inherent in free market competition, and mindful of the power of colonialization and economic neo-colonialization to forestall such crises, many capitalist economies, led by the US, have resorted to strategic interventions in supposedly free market competition. These include, collusion with asset stripping Russian oligarchs, militaristic resource grabs, and sanctions targeting regimes resistant to neo-colonialization. Additionally there has been massive government financial intervention in the market, taking the form of tariffs, bailouts, subsidies, financial guarantees, and the like, not only rendering the insistence that Chinese competitors have an unfair advantage on account of their governments support derisory, but which, resulting in substantial increases to national debt, has consequently diminished government's capacity to invest in infrastructural and technological innovation that might otherwise boost competitive production.

**Keywords** Free market abandoned • Geostrategic intervention • Economic intervention

In light of the demonstrable incapacity of economic neo-colonialization, or the globalized expansion of the free market, to accomplish what is now thus shown to be an inevitably futile attempt to overcome the ontological contradiction arising from the economic logic of competitive capitalism,



S. Glynn, *The Economic Logic of Late Capitalism and the Inevitable Triumph of Socialism*,
https://doi.org/10.1007/978-3-030-52667-2_13

the US, previously its leading exponent, has increasingly sought to *selectively* eliminate such free-market competition. For instance, in behavior not unreminiscent of the colonial monopolization of resources, by which capitalist economies, as we saw Lenin point out, traditionally managed to stave of crises of overproduction, the US, aided and abetted by institutions largely designed and set up by those such as Treasury official Larry Summers and his protégé economist Andrei Shleifer, colluded with the Russian oligarchs,[1] in the stripping of many of the resources or asset of the former USSR. An operation that, by reducing overall production costs contributed significantly to the growth of US corporate profits, and the consequent tripling of the Dow Jones Industrial Index during the decade after the collapse of the Soviet Union, from which, as demonstrated by the aforementioned fall in average wages over that period, the US working classes benefited not at all.

Perhaps encouraged by the success of this operation, the US, accompanied most supportively by the British, invaded Iraq, which was thought to have oil reserves of up to 300 Billion barrels (subsequently revised down to approximately 140 billion barrels) as compared with Saudi Arabia's estimated 250 billion barrels.[2] Indeed, in an attempt to forestall a crisis of

[1] Following the collapse of the former Soviet Union, President Boris Yeltsin, at the urging of the US, was encouraged to prop up the economy by selling off or privatizing the vast resources of a state that had presided over nine time zones; resources which, acquired by the oligarchs at fire sale prices through nefarious practices—including, but not limited to, rigged tenders and auctions, bribes, murder and ensuing treats to the apparatchiks of the bureaucracy responsible for setting the prices of such assets—could then be sold on at comparatively modest prices to the West, where they then played a significant role in fueling the US economic boom of the 1990s.

[2] Those skeptical of the claim that the invasion of Iraq was about the oil might do well to consider that the US and Britain were the two nations in the world with, at that time, and for different reasons, the greatest redundant oil extraction capacity, and, arguably, expertise, while the invasion was opposed by France, China, and Russia, which is to say the three nations with oil extraction contracts with Iraq. Furthermore, it will be remembered that, while around 30 or so corpses per day, bearing signs of the most hideous tortures, were being dumped on the streets of Baghdad, a circumstance to which US Secretary of Defense Donald Rumsfeld's response was that "Democracy is messy," the invading forces' number one priority was the securing and protection of the oil wells, and that US occupation chief Paul Bremer's first act was to pass a series of orders and laws, which the interim government was specifically prohibited from changing, opening up Iraq's oil reserves to direct foreign ownership. Clearly then, while *debatably* not a *sufficient* cause of the Iraq war, the attempt to acquire oil appears *indisputably* to have been a *necessary* condition thereof. [For a fuller account of all this see Simon Glynn, Deconstructing Terrorism, in *Philosophical Forum*

overproduction by maintaining profits even as workers' wages are subject to downward pressure, there has been a generalized scramble for diminishing resources,[3] which has increasingly resulted, if not in outright wars then in destabilizing conflicts. Thus it has not gone unnoticed that Venezuela, to whose potential regime change the current US administration has devoted so much effort, is believed to have oil reserves of almost 300 billion barrels; more than those of Saudi Arabia, and more than twice those of Iraq. And surely no one imagines the ongoing violence in Libya to be unconnected to the fact that it has the largest oil deposits in Africa. While belatedly waking up to the increased activity of China and other nations in negotiating long-term contracts for African resources, the US, responding in typical militaristic fashion, established Africa Command, apparently portending an increased reversion back to some form of colonialization, however it will undoubtedly attempt to disguise it!

Nor, of course, has it been only with regard to resource grabs that the US and other leading economies have suspended the principles of free-market competition. Indeed as we have already seen the US government's bailing out of GM and Chevrolet, not to mention GM affiliated GMAC, as well as the American International Group AIG, Bear Sterns, and a host of other financial institutions, was clearly a form of corporate welfare. And although GM, GMAC, and Chrysler eventually paid back much of what they received, they still came up $10.2 billion short, even excluding interest. However this pales into insignificance in comparison to the $700 billion Troubled Asset Relief Program (TARP), while it represents a rounding error when taken in conjunction with the Treasury Department's $3.757 trillion Money Market Mutual Fund (MMMF), $1 trillion Public-Private Investment Fund, $400 billion Government-Sponsored Enterprise (GSE) stock purchase, $314 billion, GSE backed, securities purchases,

*Quarterly*, vol. xxxvi, No.1. Spring 2005, pp. 113–128. See also, Chapter 19, footnote 3.] while the recent abandoning of Kurdish forces, one of the US's closest allies in the fight against the Islamic State, in Northern Syria, to a Turkish, anti-Kurdish, military offensive, and the subsequent return of US troops to Eastern Syria where most of Syria's oil fields are, can leave little doubt as to US priorities and motivation.

[3] Including, but by no means limited to, fossil fuel resources, which will surely be replaced by ambient solar, wind, wave, tidal, current, and more conventional hydroelectric, energy resources as soon as the power of vested interests in the oil, gas, and coal industries to influence political decision-making is diminished, as it is surely already on the verge of being, as—despite the capacity of the fossil fuel industry to externalize so much of its real costs, nevertheless—many renewables become cheaper than fossil fuels.

$301 billion City Group asset guarantee and $260 billion Fed funding T-bill action, as well as the Federal Reserve's $1.8 trillion Commercial Paper Funding Facility, $1.25 trillion Mortgage backed securities purchase, $1 trillion Term Asset Backed Securities Loan Facility, $755 billion Foreign central bank currency liquidity swaps, $540 billion Money Market investor Funding facility, $300 billion Treasury purchase program, $200 billion GSE program, $148 billion Private Dealer Credit Facility, $146 billion Asset Backed Commercial Paper MMMF liquidity facility, $138 billion to J.P. Morgan Chase/Lehman Brothers, $125 billion Tri-party repurchase agreements, $125 billion Open Market Operations, and a host of other lesser loans and guarantees in the $13–80 billion range, to an actual total of over $14 trillion.[4] Not unlike FDR'S New Deal in the wake of the Wall Street Crash, and post-WWII Marshall Aid, that saved and promoted capitalism, these later government interventions clearly sacrificed the supposedly free market to what unarguably amounts to publically funded or underwritten, and thus socialist, bailouts of, and other massive government financial assistance to, capitalist corporations and the like. Government interventions in light of which the trade war with China and others, entailing as it does the imposition of tariffs in further opposition to the free market, on the grounds that *their* governments unfairly deviate from free-market principles by supporting their industries, is as laughable as it is ludicrous.

Indeed, notwithstanding their disingenuous espousal of anti-government rhetoric, capitalists and their cohorts have worked assiduously to have their governments intervene, on their behalf, in the economy. However given the fact that they nevertheless remain unprepared to abandon their competitive ethos, or to give up the privileges of ownership, not only has such intervention, and the *crony* capitalism[5] that is fast becoming the only surviving form of the species, been palpably *unjust*, even by capitalism's own lax standards, but in any event it has met with extremely *limited success*.

To the first point first, regarding injustice, to the cost to taxpayers of TARP one must, of course, add the cost of the Fed's indirect control over

[4] See Nomi Prins, *It Takes a Pillager*, Hoboken, NJ: Wiley, 2009.

[5] Crony capitalism, in that, as we have seen, much of the wealth accruing to the economic elite derives from their capacity to influence the political elite, and therefore to ensure state intervention on their behalf, in exchange for campaign contributions, not to mention consultancy fees, revolving door appointments and the like.

the Federal Funds Rate and so on, which artificially lowered interest rates to small savers invested in Treasury Bonds, regular Money Markets, and the like. While to the second point, regarding limited success, although it is to be admitted that there was an upside to such behavior, such as the saving of GM and Chrysler—not to mention, *if one is committed to capitalism*, a slew of banking and other financial institutions which constitute its (consequently again beating) heart—nevertheless, given that, as we saw, the ongoing survival of these automobile corporations in a competitive economy required a severe reduction in wages and other benefits, which translated into a reduction in aggregate demand, then it has only been by a combination of the Fed's Quantitative Easing, and its capacity to hold down interest rates, which is to say by re-inflating the credit bubble, that the government has thus been able to artificially stimulate demand to a sufficient level to avoid a slide back into recession. And we have all seen the long-term consequences of such inflationary bubbles!

Furthermore, even were we to allow that this time the *domestic* credit bubble might be sufficiently well managed to prevent it from bursting, the long-term capacity of the US government to manage its capitalist economy in such ways is entirely problematic. For, even granted that the US economy—*exceptionally* by virtue of its size, the *supposed* transparency,[6] its fiat currency, the status of its currency as a reserve currency, and its nomination of its international debt obligations in US dollars (which provided incentives for those to whom it owed money to support the US dollar)—was widely considered the *least bad* financial haven during the Great Recession, and was, as a consequence, fortuitously insulated from the enormously inflationary and other adverse financial effects normally resulting from the aforementioned policies, its capacity to indulge in such behavior is nevertheless ultimately limited by its cost. Thus although the government may, by employing TARP and other financial instruments, write down or otherwise cover debt incurred by banks and other financial institutions due to their overextension of credit to consumers with no realistic long-term ability to pay it off, its capacity to do so ultimately comes at a considerable cost. A cost which if it is not to be met by increased

[6] The bogusness of this claim was never made more clearly apparent than it was by the great recession, where the "Triple A" ratings given to wholly inferior securitized debt obligations, and the extensive hedging, via credit default swaps, and so on, against the massive risk this implied, were, or at least so we are told and encouraged to believe, apparently entirely unrecognized even by regulators, much less investors!

taxes, which would simply suppress the very demand that many of these costs were incurred in order to stimulate in the first place, or by the sale of assets (of which more later), must be met by government borrowing; US National Debt standing, even prior to the coronavirus pandemic, at over $23.5 trillion or approximately 106% of GDP, which is to say about $70,000 per head, *well over a Quarter of a Million Dollars for a family of 4* (more than the median cost of a house in the US) and slated, even before the coronavirus pandemic, to rise by over $1 trillion, or around 5%, per year, well ahead of even the then projected growth, over the next few years! A strategy which must ultimately result in a massive *debt funding obligation* which, in addition to itself suppressing the very *demand* that such borrowing was designed to stimulate, will leave less and less to invest in potentially *supply* boosting technological and other economic infrastructure that might, by increasing productivity, enable the economy to emerge from such debt! A debt obligation, and concomitant demand suppression, which is almost insignificant when compared to around $124 trillion in unfunded liabilities[7] with which the US economy is currently burdened!

[7] Unfunded US liabilities include such demand stimulants as Social Security, veterans and federal employees' benefits and Medicare, as well as publically held federal debt.

CHAPTER 14

# From Crony Capitalism to Strategic Research and Development Investment, and Back Again

**Abstract** Mainly protective and reactive, current *government* financial intervention is contrasted with its more immediately post-war *investment in technology boosting Research and Development*. Investment that ushered in a technological revolution which, *absent* effective *competition* from other, recently war-torn, advanced economies enabled the financing of The Great Society program of enhanced welfare benefits, and from which R&D many major private corporations still benefit enormously. *Government investment more usually characteristic, especially in the absence of competition, of socialist economies*, which was largely scaled back by economic neo-liberals. Particularly unfortunate timing, coinciding as it did with the recovery of previously war-torn, largely government funded, competitors. Facts which invite comparison between the potential benefits of non-competitive government funded, and therefore essentially socialist, and privately funded and competitive, essentially capitalist, economies.

**Keywords** Research and development • Great society • Government investment • Non-competitive • Competitive

It would be wrong to assume that government intervention in the supposedly free-market economy has been limited to the aforementioned corporate welfare, direct bailouts, loan guarantees, tariffs, and other similar corporate assistance, not to mention resource grabs. For indeed, the US



S. Glynn, *The Economic Logic of Late Capitalism and the Inevitable Triumph of Socialism*,
https://doi.org/10.1007/978-3-030-52667-2_14

government, anxious, in the wake of WWII, to maintain US technological superiority and all the benefits that flowed from it, markedly increased its investment in Research and Development (R&D) from $940 million or 2.4% of government expenditure in 1949 to 13.8 billion, or 11.7% by 1965, as, non-coincidently US median income rose substantially, fueled in considerable part by "the white heat of technology" as then Prime Minister Harold Wilson referred to similar developments in the UK. Thus it was estimated that US government investment accounted for approximately 85% of R&D in the US electronics industry for example, much of which benefited major US corporations such as IBM, Sperry, Burroughs, and Control Data.[1]

However, the "Keynesian Consensus" driven government investment linked to demand stimulation, so successful in driving post-war US economic growth that brought unprecedented economic prosperity to the middle classes, and rendered Lyndon Johnson's Great Society package of enhanced welfare benefits possible, gave way at the very beginning of the 1980s to the ideology of *laissez-faire* or free-market economic neo-liberalism,[2] which, with its austerity programs reigning in government

[1] See Leffler, M.R. 2012. Cold War Lessons for the GOP. *The Nation.*, November 12, p. 17.

[2] *Economic neo-liberals ostensibly oppose all government intervention in the economy as a restriction of "freedom" as they define or interpret it as* the *Freedom* of capitalists *To* maximize their profits by ignoring the environmental, health, and social consequences of their exploitation of the environment and workforce. A definition which, of course, fails to consider the Freedom of the general public, and workers, *From* the life and property threatening effects of sea level rise, increasing cyclones or hurricanes, flooding, drought, and other catastrophic weather events resulting from the effects of anthropogenic global climate change, pollution by industrial toxins, and the dangers emanating from inadequate protection of health and safety in the workplace. Nor does it consider *freedom* from extreme poverty and other effects of low wages and unemployment, and the inability of a government to provide healthcare, education and basic housing and food, and thus *freedom from* preventable disease, preventable ignorance, homelessness, and starvation, for the poor as a consequence of giving corporations and the economic elite, tax breaks, and so on. Furthermore, and equally *significantly in the above context, restriction of government investment in technological R&D helps ensure that so far from the financial and numerous other benefits of technological innovation being, at least potentially, publically available to some extent to all, they be largely focused upon, if not entirely restricted to, benefiting those already extremely wealthy individuals and corporations with the financial capacity who/which, absent government investment, are free to monopolize the benefits of technological development to their own advantage. A strategy which, by rejecting the massive resources available to government, tends, and contra neo-liberal ideology, to hold back, rather than accelerate, the rate of aggregated technological advancement!*

spending on or support of *general* R&D, resulted in stagnant demand and recession. Particularly unfortunate coming as it did just as the Western European, especially West German, together with Japanese, economies and technologies, initially buoyed by Marshall Aid and the like, and subsequently buoyed by continuing investment by these countries' own governments, caught up and began to outcompete the US in a number of industries. Although due to the restrictions placed on West Germany and Japan under the post-WWII terms of treaty, weapons, and other military technologies and their industries were not among them. It tellingly being precisely continuing US government investment in and spending on *military* technology—which despite standing in stark contradiction to the neo-liberalism to which they are ostensibly so committed, Republicans and some others are, none the less, so active in promoting[3]—which, in producing the internet, in conjunction with the microchip, semiconductors, and computers, subsequently enabled Microsoft, Google, Facebook, Amazon, and Apple, and a number of other US corporations operating in internet related fields, to become and remain unrivaled, and *individual* entrepreneurs like Bill Gates, Mark Zuckerberg, Jeff Bezos, Steve Jobs and a host of other dot com Billionaires and lesser camp followers to make huge, *private*, fortunes.

Thus whether in the US, West Germany, Japan, or, following them, South Korea, Brazil, India, it has largely been government lead and/or enhanced—even if not always government sustained—investment of public money which has been responsible for what is therefore largely *socialist* investment, that has enabled, if not entire national economies, then at least leading corporations, to become and remain highly profitable, even while paying their corporate workforces sufficiently well to ensure that they helped maintain a buoyant demand for their products, and thus the very profitability which, to come full circle, makes all of this possible. Which helps to explain why, unlike most of the rest of the Euro Zone, Germany for example, as a beneficiary of much such, continuing, government investment, has not had to borrow or avail itself of credit in order to avoid a crisis of overproduction, and has consequently not suffered the

[3] Presumably explicable not only by the desire of the wealthy, whose economic interests' neo-liberalism largely reflects, to protect their assets, but also by the authoritarian personality type of so many economic neo-liberals.

economic meltdown or Great Recession, that beset so many of its neighbors.[4]

But let us not forget of course, that whatever short-term success such technological investment—and the resultant capacity to produce goods and/or services of a ***type or sort, or/and quality***, or/and with an ***efficiency*** that others could not match—has thus made possible, it remains the case that *insofar and to the degree that these economies are and remain truly competitive* then clearly the elevation or success of any of them must be at the expense of the others, which is to say a zero-sum affair, as the decline of the US auto industry in the face of Japanese, German, and South Korean competition, clearly demonstrated. A trend that was, as we have seen, only arrested to the extent that General Motors and Chevrolet were bailed out at the bottom of the recession by the US government which, thereby enabling the development of competitive technologies and new models, resulted in their being able to manufacture products of a comparable *sort* and somewhat competitive *quality*, at a competitive *price*. An instance of government and thus publically funded, or *socialist*, "corporate welfare," by virtue of which the US auto industry was able to compete with, similarly government funded, foreign auto manufacturers. And although it is true that competition, albeit government funded rather than capitalist, has, in this case at least, spurred technological innovation, this same competition has also, as previously noted, put downward pressure on the wages and benefits of US auto workers, to the point where, post the Great Recession, new employees have had to accept greatly reduced pay and benefit packages, thus limiting their subsequent economic demand. It only being trade union strike solidarity that has made some headway in ameliorating this situation to a limited extent.

And as with the auto industry, so too, of course, with technological innovation in general. In other words, *while such innovation may, by enabling those who invest in it to produce goods of a* ***sort*** *or/and* ***quality*** *or/and with an* ***efficiency*** *that others may, temporarily at least, be unable to match, within a competitive, which is to say a zero-sum (win/lose), system the gains of one or more economies or corporations—and thus potentially the*

[4] Nor do the travails that first beset the Japanese economy in the 1990s provide a counter example to the wisdom of such investment in technology, as the stock market crash there, so far from being the result of an overextension of credit to *consumers* (or demand side stimulus) was the consequence of an overextension of credit to Japanese *corporations* (supply side stimulus) and subsequent attempts to check the *asset* price bubble it fueled by a sharp rise in inter-bank lending rates.

*wages, benefits, and concomitant increase in aggregate demand—will be at the expense of another or others. Moreover as others catch up it can clearly be seen to result in a lose/lose situation, or race to the bottom, as each competes against the others, by lowering wages and benefits, and thus aggregate demand, while increasing output, thereby inevitably resulting in a crisis of overproduction.*[5] *A circumstance that not only raises, but pushes to the fore, the question of whether, and if so how, the increased efficiency and capacities resulting from investment in technology can benefit humanity in general, as surely it not only morally should, but pragmatically must if the economy, and the society dependent upon it, are to survive the aforementioned crisis?*

[5] To explicate it more precisely, and from a slightly different perspective, in a competitive capitalist system, assuming risks are comparable, investment will flow to where it can obtain the greatest return, which is to say to where it is most productive in the narrow, economic, sense of maximizing the ratio of the ***value of outputs or products*** as a proportion of the ***cost of inputs*** such as ***demand*** stimulating wages and benefits and so on. The gap between output and demand thus becoming ever greater as one moves from less competitive to more competitive economies. Thus to switch investments from the less productive to the more productive, or in other words from the less economically efficient to the more economically efficient, in pursuit of maximum profitability, by thus widening the gap between economic supply and demand, as one is bound to do in an entirely profit driven, competitive capitalist system, merely exacerbates the problem of overproduction.

CHAPTER 15

# The Moral Limitations and Pragmatic Dangers to the Environment, Health, and the Economy of Technological Innovation, Under Capitalism

**Abstract** Survival in a *truly* competitive environment requires *maximizing* efficiency, which is to say the ratio of outputs over inputs, or profitability, which entails *taking* the *most* possible *from*, while *contributing* the *least* possible *to*, labor and the physical and socio-cultural environment, and also externalizing as many costs as possible. This, in addition to maximizing the exploitation of labor, thereby resulting in a crisis of overproduction, results in environmental degradation. While conversely, any contribution made by capitalist enterprises, as opposed to technology, to general welfare, which they survive, must be indicative of a lack of competition. Moreover, absent government investment, the preponderance of the benefits of the increased productivity generally characteristic of ever more complex, and expensive, technologies, will increasingly accrue, uncontested, to the wealthy, thereby, as *per* Thomas Piketty, leading to ever-greater economic inequality.

**Keywords** Productivity • Efficiency • Profitability • Exploitation • Inequality • Environmental degradation • Piketty

As previously noted, post-war US government investment in technological R&D was substantial, reaching 11.7% of government expenditure in 1965. And while the subsequent neo-liberal role-back of such government investment, entailing, as it did, the rejection of the massive resources



S. Glynn, *The Economic Logic of Late Capitalism and the Inevitable Triumph of Socialism*,
https://doi.org/10.1007/978-3-030-52667-2_15

available to government for investment in such innovation, thereby slowed down aggregated technological advancement from which all might have benefited, it ensured, as intended, that much of the technological innovation that nevertheless did take place would, rather than merely contingently enabling profit-generating spin-offs, instead specifically focus upon promoting the interests, financial and otherwise, of those private individuals and capitalist corporations with the financial capacity to back it. However, although the financial elite thus effectively monopolize many of the benefits derived from technological innovation, if they are to survive as such in a *truly free and transparent competitive market supposedly characteristic of laissez-faire* capitalism, they are compelled to submit to its rule, and consequently to invest in whatever maximizes the interest or/and dividends deriving therefrom, at the expense of all else. For clearly, to do otherwise will, other things being equal, simply render them *uncompetitive* in comparison to those who, in doing so, will undercut their pricing in the market and *attract capital investment away from them.*

Under such conditions then not only are the financial elite and their corporations constrained to finance or invest only in those activities and projects and so on that generate *positive* profits or returns but—as if this were not sufficient to bar investment in *most* social welfare, environmental and other, similar, projects—they are further constrained, if they wish to compete successfully against their rivals, to invest in those enterprises, activities, projects, and so on, which *maximize the ratio of the value of outputs or production, over inputs or costs*, and concomitantly such profits or returns. Which is usually to say enterprises, activities, projects which *contribute the least to*—even to the extent of externalizing as many of their costs as possible—*while taking the most they can from, the environment and society at large!* Thus, for instance, the paying of anything above subsistence wages, investment in social welfare projects such as those associated with care for any of the young, the aged or the chronically ill, support for the creation or/and maintenance of pleasant social spaces and interactions, and the like, investment in culturally fulfilling activities and events, or in the reducing or reversing of environmental degradation, pollution, and so on, indeed any investment which reduces, or does not result in, the greatest possible productivity or return on investment, is clearly inimical to economic survival in a *truly transparent and competitive free market.* A circumstance which will not only maximize the exploitation of labor, resulting in crises of overproduction, and ultimately in free market capitalism's demise, but will also result in the exploitation and degradation of the physical, social, and cultural environments in the process. In which case, perhaps counterintuitively, so far from any contribution that capitalist enterprises have made, over the years, to general wellbeing demonstrating its potential for munificence, insofar as such contributions were not instrumental in profit optimization, they can only have been sustained as a consequence of the lack of the market "freedom" and/or transparency and/or—as in the case of Johnson's Great Society for example—lack of competition!

Furthermore, insofar as the technologies we do develop are usually increasingly complex and/or large scale, then they generally require access to ever greater amounts of capital, which, absent government involvement will tend to enable the already wealthy to effectively monopolize the most advanced, and therefore most productive or profitable, sectors of the economy;[1] which is to say to profit from the increase in output and reduction in wages, that technological innovation enables. A fact which, together with the aforementioned imperative to maximize profitability, will result in the already rich getting ever richer, thereby enhancing their capacity to further monopolize *the most profitable market sectors, and so on*. The top 1% deriving over half their income from capital gains and dividends. The possession and accumulation of capital thus becomes a self-reinforcing cause and consequence of the continuing ability of those who already have substantial capital and concomitant power to accumulate more of both. Which helps explain why, as Thomas Piketty has pointed out,[2] return on capital (r) outpaces overall growth (g) in the economy (r > g) and economic inequality becomes ever more pronounced.

Given that the undoubted capacity and corresponding propensity of the wealthy, who are inevitably the major beneficiaries of this *return* on capital, to save a greater proportion of their income than the less wealthy wage earners, and thus to accumulate more capital—to the point where, as already mentioned, the top 1% of the US population now own more wealth than the bottom 90%—then as Piketty recognizes, and as per our analysis throughout, this will eventually result in a reduction in the very aggregate demand that technological innovation might otherwise have

[1] Thus, although it is true that Bill Gates and others generated much profit without, initially at least, investing much capital, their success was, of course, as previously mentioned, dependent upon massive *government* investment in the internet, and the development of the microchip, the semiconductor, and computers.

[2] See Thomas Piketty, *Capitalism in the Twentieth Century* (Cambridge, MA: Harvard University Press, 2014).

stimulated, thereby portending the crisis of overproduction, and consequently the treat to the very survival of capitalism, which it was hoped that technology would mitigate. Or, to explicate the above more fully, insofar as both wages and the return on capital, or profits, are to be derived from gross sales revenues, then increasing dependence on technology and technological innovation, requiring, as it normally does, increased capital investment, will, in a capitalist economy, enable the already wealthy corporations and individuals to effectively monopolize the most productive and profitable sectors, and, other things being equal, result in an increase in the overall return on capital, or profits, and thus capital accumulation. An increase in return which, coming as it does from gross sales revenue, will be at the expense of wages and benefits, and therefore of the demand-derived therefrom. A fact demonstrated by the previously mentioned doubling of US GDP and 18-fold increase in the Dow Jones Index between 1982 and 2007 even as the median income fell by over 30%, precipitating the crisis of overproduction that manifested itself as the Great Recession. This then adding a *pragmatic* concern to the *moral* concerns that many increasingly have, regarding the wide, and widening, inequality resulting from increasing capital accumulation.

CHAPTER 16

# The Regulatory Response to Globalized Free-Market Capitalist Competition, and the Free Rider Strategy as Antithetical to Technological Innovation and Education

**Abstract** Previously, investment in R&D resulted in increasingly *productive* technologies, and/or in the ability to make goods of a *quality* and/or *sort* others could not, which enabled advanced economies to pay wages sufficient to defer or ameliorate crises of overproduction. However, technological development also facilitated the free flow of technological information and expertise, rendering such advantages increasingly problematic and transient. Consequently, capitalists have increasingly abandoned free market competition, which they formerly asserted was a spur to investment in R&D, in favor of ever more stringent patent and copyright restrictions, tariffs, and opposition to others' international mergers and acquisitions of expertise and so on, and even deferred some investment in technology and advanced education, in favor of *their* investment in mergers and "brain draining" acquisition of others' technology and expertise. A "free rider" contradiction of Adam Smith's assertion that the pursuit of each of their self-interest is to the mutual advantage of all.

**Keywords** Free rider • Adam Smith refuted • Technological insulation eroded • Free market abandoned

In contrast to colonization and economic neo-colonialism, which helped ease downward pressure on the wages of workers in the colonizing countries, at the *expense* of, if not always necessarily to the immediate *detriment*



S. Glynn, *The Economic Logic of Late Capitalism and the Inevitable Triumph of Socialism*,
https://doi.org/10.1007/978-3-030-52667-2_16

of,[1] the colonized, advances in transportation and information technology, and the increasing *frictionless flow of resources, labor, information, expertize and the resulting advanced technologies*—characteristic of the "Flat World" as Thomas Friedman has dubbed the globalization resulting from such advances—has drastically inhibited the capacity to *monopolize* techniques or/and technologies that are capable of greater ***productivity***, *or of producing goods and/or services of a* ***type*** *or* ***quality*** *that others cannot.* A development that has not only progressively brought workers in previously underdeveloped and developing countries into proximate competition with those in developed countries, thereby putting downward pressure on the latter's wages, but also rendering the *competitive* advantage and *financial returns* to be gained from investment in technological R&D increasingly problematic and transient. Developments which have increasingly limited, if not reduced, many of the advantages previously enjoyed by the advanced economies. The much lauded efficiency of the globalized free market therefore posing an ever greater threat to the hitherto more developed economies. Consequently, having championing the "free market" when they benefited from it, capitalists in these economies, and their representatives in government, have shown little hesitation in turning around and attempting to restricting it, as the US administration's trade war with China clearly demonstrates.

Indeed, many observers believe that the US administration's attempt to restrict adoption of Huawei's 5G technology primarily stems not, as claimed, from security concerns, but from economic concerns. And where they have been less successful in restricting the free market, the previously more developed economies have encountered fierce competition. For instance, no longer limited to providing call center services, or even banking advice, India is currently offering legal services online, while it is by no means uncommon for citizens of the US and other advanced economies to fly to India or other developing nations, for non-emergency surgery and other medical treatments. And turning from the provision of services to the production of goods, although Samsung has had much success in adopting elements of Apple's I-Phone technology, and the endless patent disputes between Apple and Motorola are indicative of a similar attempt by the one to benefit from the technology developed by the other, the

[1] The distinction I wish to draw is that between the undoubted exploitation of the colonized, by the colonizers, and the fact that colonization may nevertheless, in some cases, improved the living standards of the colonized.

latest Chinese Xiaomi smart phone, which, adopting much of its technology from others, is now said to be best of all.

Nor is the "frictionless flow" of technologies limited to the illicit piracy of intellectual property, or the ignoring or circumventing of copyright or patent protections and the like, for it may equally be the result of legal acquisitions and mergers, such as Chinese registered Lenovo's acquisition of the personal computer division of IBM.[2] The very *direct* investment in technological R&D, initially incentivized by *competition*, increasingly becoming disincentivized by such competition in favor of *indirect* investment via financial mergers and acquisitions made possible by a free market, that enables the buying up of the competition and its expertize. Clearly then, such consequences of a free market will, if unchecked, increasingly result in competitive capitalist economies withholding much investment in technological R&D, as each attempts to become a "free rider" on the backs of the others. The very *competition* which capitalists assure us is a spur to investment in R&D, and thus the development of the technology efficiencies and capacities derived therefrom, becoming in the context of a globalized economy *that technological development itself has enabled*,[3] a disincentive to such future investment in technological R&D, just as it has to tax-funded government investment in "education" or job training. Why, after all, invest heavily in R&D in pursuit of innovative technologies, if one can derive advanced technologies and information from one's competitors, or indeed in the education facilitating such R&D, or even in the degree level training of a domestic workforce, when by waiting for one's competitors to do so one can reap the extensive competitive benefits derivable therefrom almost immediately by "Brain Draining" graduates and postgraduates, who have been largely educated at the expense of other economies.[4] A "double whammy" in that not only does it save the

[2] Although IBM's move may be couched in terms of the "rising tide" argument, *viz.* that it was in fact an example of abandoning previously developed, simpler computers, in order to concentrate upon the "greener pastures" offered by the development of more advanced super computers and the like, in light of the argument unfolding here it will hopefully become increasingly clear that any advantage which such a strategy may afford can itself only be temporary.

[3] Thus, the microchip and the internet, together with the container ship and other transportation technologies, have clearly been major constitutive elements of globalization.

[4] Although it is true that the US, for example, has leading technological research institutions like CalTech and MIT, a large proportion of the students, particularly at graduate level, are foreign nationals and a large proportion of the faculty are naturalized US citizens.

wealthier, advanced economies, to which skilled labor often gravitates, the cost of extensive investment in such education themselves but, in thus robbing the poorer, less advanced, economies, of the skilled labor emigrating from them, it also diminishes *their* potential competitiveness! And although it is true that the tide can flow both ways as demonstrated by the free flow of highly skilled computer engineers and technicians, often *returning* to India from European and US graduate schools, thereby facilitating the growth of computing and information technologies in Bangalore, for example,[5] this in no way diminishes, but indeed exemplifies, the increasingly ephemeral nature of any *competitive* (as opposed to socially cooperative) advantage to be gained from direct investment in the real economy, whether in technological hardware, or the development of technological skills and competencies.

*In what then amounts to another, albeit in this case perversely inverted, example of the failure of Adam Smith's invisible or hidden hand, if each pursues their own self-interest, then the increasingly frictionless flow of advanced technologies, information, and technical expertise characteristic of a globalized free market may well, at least in its competitive capitalist as opposed to co-operative socialist form, have the overall effect of reducing or stifling investment in technological R&D, and "education," to the mutual disadvantage of all.*

*Thus just as Marx foresaw that free-market competition would put downward pressure on both profits and wages, thereby threatening capitalism's long-term survival, so similarly an increasingly "flat" world renders the competitive advantage and profitability deriving from direct investment in the very technological innovation and expertise which—by increasing productivity and/or the quality, and/or the sort of goods and/or services being produced—might otherwise have helped support profits and wages, and thus*

[5] The reasons for this are numerous, but the most significant is surely that Indian companies, and indeed companies in many of the emerging economies, have offered returning graduates very generous "stock options," enabling them to reap enormous rewards, particularly in the case of successful "start-ups" and small companies characteristic of such economies, for which even modest economic success represents a far higher percentage of their relatively low initial capital value, than would similar growth of initially much larger companies. And in the case of socialist or communist economies, Chinese government officials, for example, routinely offer Chinese nationals, and naturalized former Chinese nationals working in any number of US and other university research departments, impressive research facilities, support and wages, in order to incentivize them to return to China to work for the Chinese economy.

*staved off any impending crisis of overproduction, increasingly problematic. While returning to, and advancing, the theme of the previous chapter, even if the increasing capital investment necessary, in an increasingly technologically complex world, to promote significant technological innovation, is forthcoming, the usually increasing proportion of gross revenues necessary to pay the interest on such investment, or/and the increasingly large profit necessary to incentivize it—much of which profit, as previously argued, is saved—divert money away from wages, and reduces the very demand which such investment must satisfy to remain profitable.*

CHAPTER 17

# The Alternative: The Pragmatic and Moral Advantages of Globalized Socialist Cooperation

**Abstract** Socialist economies, rejecting competitive profitability in favor of cooperation by which all benefit from the progress of each, consequently eschew "free rider," development inhibiting, strategies. Furthermore, unlike competitive economies' wasteful duplication and dispersion of R&D expertise, socialisms' cooperative ethos pools it to great synergistic effect. Moreover, unconstrained by competition and profit maximization, as soon as the most basic material needs are met socialism moves to enhance worker, and general social and environmental, welfare; remaining surpluses being reinvested in economic growth. Thus, notwithstanding the introduction of profit taking to motivate production in some non-essential economic areas, the direct reinvestment of surplus in the other areas further contributes to the dynamic growth of the Chinese economy; development in the USSR falling victim to an arms race.

**Keywords** Wasteful duplication • Synergistic • Infrastructure • Worker and environmental welfare

In contrast to capitalist economies, socialist economies being, *at least insofar as they are not in* ***competition*** *with capitalist economies,* ***cooperative—all thereby benefiting from the progress made by each****—have no reason, as do competitive capitalists in a free market, to hold back on investment and attempt to catch a "free ride"; no reason to thereby slow technological*



S. Glynn, *The Economic Logic of Late Capitalism and the Inevitable Triumph of Socialism*,
https://doi.org/10.1007/978-3-030-52667-2_17

*innovation and economic growth, for fear of loss of private competitiveness or/and profitability vis-à-vis those who may attempt to derive a "free ride" at their expense. Nor, insofar as they are unconcerned with competitive profitability, are they inhibited by the logic of capitalism from investing in environmental and welfare programs, and the like, aimed at promoting general* ***social wellbeing or utility****. Rather, on the contrary, they are both* ***pragmatically*** *free and* ***ideologically*** *or* ***morally*** *inclined, to do so, even if unfortunately sometimes at the indisputable cost of individual rights.*[1] *Moreover, in cutting out profit taking from the return on their investments they reduce the expense of technological R&D and ensure that if not all, then a large proportion, of the wealth generated thereby is directly funneled back into the real economy, thereby stimulating supply side investment, which rather than being used to increase profits may be used to enable increasing demand side wages and benefits. All of which factors, in addition to helping accelerate the pace of technological innovation, as well as fending off any potential crisis of overproduction, ensures that, other things being equal, socialist economies have the potential to grow much more rapidly than do their capitalist counterparts.*

*And as if all of this were not impressive enough, unlike capitalist economies, in which competition results in wasteful duplication of R&D as well as the dispersion of research expertise into any number of competitive companies or corporations, socialist economies can foster cooperative R&D, bringing expertise together to great synergistic effect, as well as other, more obvious, advantage.* Indeed it was surely precisely in recognition of the potential efficiency of cooperative as opposed to competitive R&D, that when the "chips were

[1] Thus, as analysis of Utilitarian ethics, for instance, reveals, the pursuit of general wellbeing, or in the case of Utilitarianism, more specifically, the "sum total of human happiness," not infrequently finds itself in tension with the upholding of individual rights. While, as the notion of Eminent Domain in the US, as well as, more generally, enforced quarantine in an attempt to stem the coronavirus epidemic demonstrates, many governments committed to capitalist principles, and usually willing to stand up for the individual's relatively unconstrained right or *positive freedom to* act in his/her own interests—even at the cost of the common social or communal good or *negative freedom from* the potentially deleterious impact of such unconstrained rights—are, under some circumstances, prepared to override individual rights in the name of general social or communal utility or wellbeing. The differences in the relative weight given to individual rights in relation to overall social or community wellbeing, often, although clearly not always, being as much dependent upon the *nature* of the rights and wellbeing in question, as upon the *degree* to which the one may take precedence over the other. [For a much fuller explication of the differences between positive and negative freedom see Sir Isaiah Berlin, *Two Concepts of Liberty* (Oxford: Clarendon Press, 1958)].

down" The Manhattan Project's research into and development of nuclear weapons technology was government funded, unitraly organized, and directed, as indeed was the National Aeronautics and Space Administration (NASA),[2] along with the *initial* development of internet technology by the military, much, as previously noted, to subsequent US corporate advantage. And all of the aforementioned benefits derivable from socialism, are certainly no less pronounced under communism; and this regardless of whether or not one agrees on what individual freedoms should be limited, and to what degree, in the name of overall social utility.[3]

Thus, surprising as it will undoubtedly seem to many, *growth rates* in the Soviet Union, fueled not only by its own form of colonial or neo-colonial exploitation of "Iron Curtain" countries, but by *government funded, organized and controlled R&D, unburdened by the capitalist imperative either of profit generation or profit taking, were much greater than in the capitalist West.*[4] A point exemplified if not demonstrated by, for instance, the fact that the nations of what would become the Soviet Union managed to go from being predominantly feudal, or quasi-feudal, agricultural societies at the time of the Russian Revolution in 1917, to being, as the USSR, the first into Space, with Sputnik, within 40 years.[5] Although given that much of its investment was directed to the development of military technologies in order to counter the threat perceived to be emanating from a hostile capitalist adversary—which not only already had nuclear weapons, but had, in bombing Nagasaki and Hiroshima, shown itself to be prepared to use them against civilian populations—this growth did not translate into as significant economic development in other areas as it otherwise surely would have, nor therefore into a vast increase in domestic consumption, as it has in China. The eventual collapse of the Soviet economy, despite its rapid economic growth, being in large part[6] due to the

[2] Note that although the bailout of GM and Chrysler was government funded, and thus socialist corporate welfare, unlike the Manhattan Project and NASA, the aforementioned capitalist corporations maintained control over the organization and direction of their government funded technological R&D.

[3] See *Ibid.*

[4] See Leffler, *op. cit.* (Chaper 14, footnote 1) p. 18.

[5] While it is to be acknowledged that this particular development was to some extent facilitated by German scientists working, post-WWII in the USSR, it should not be forgotten that the West, and in particular the US, availed itself of, at the very least, comparable, German expertise.

[6] Thus, in addition to the stress put on the Soviet system by the need to devote so much of its economic capacity to the production of armaments to defend itself, the increasingly evi-

economic burden of an arms race, strategically imposed on the USSR economically devastated by WWII[7] by the US whose economy had benefited, as we have seen, from massive growth-stimulating Allied demand for its products during that period.

Turning to China, although it is certainly true that, returning to the previously outlined de facto obstacles to economic development, unlike the colonized or neo-colonized economies, China's political elite were in no way dependent upon overseas patrons to maintain them in power, and consequently did not have an incentive to collude with them in the suppression of wage levels and resource prices, nevertheless it is certainly to be acknowledged that, not unlike capitalist profit takers, *some* Communist Party members benefited disproportionately from improvements in the national economy. However their levels of conspicuous consumption never approached those characteristic of many of the political or economic elites in lots of developing, or even undeveloped, countries. While premier Xi Jinping's recently crackdown on corruption at even the highest levels has been significant enough to continue to limit, and even to substantially reduce, corruption, as well as to prevent the investment of any great percentage of whatever disproportionate benefits accrued to Party members in foreign economies. Furthermore, although, in accordance with Deng Xiaoping's "Socialism with Chinese Characteristics," *China* has, particularly when interacting with competitive, not to say predatory, capitalist economies, certainly incorporated some aspects of the **competitive** free market into its economy, nevertheless, no matter whether motivated by principled *idealism* or in a *pragmatic* attempt to avoid any crisis of overproduction which may undermine their legitimacy, or both,[8] the Chinese

dent corruption within the political class lead, from about the mid-1960s onward, to a legitimation crisis; workers who had previously been prepared to work hard and make great sacrifices in the name of social solidarity, becoming increasingly self-interested and ever less prepared to do so.

[7] Indeed, the joke going around Washington at the time was that while the arms race had bankrupted one economy, it had come close to bankrupting two.

[8] Note that these *idealistic* and *pragmatic* motives for a more equal sharing of wealth may not, as much Western commentary has implied, necessarily be mutually exclusive. For if the communist leadership seeks to maintain its legitimacy, and thus remain in power, in order to proceed further upon the course of reducing poverty, and increasing the material wellbeing of an increasing proportion of its citizenry, then the pragmatic desire to achieve the former is in no way antithetical to the idealistic desire to achieve the latter; the relationship between the two thus being a mutually reinforcing, virtuous, circle!

government has remained committed to the communist ideology of the Communist Party of China (CPC) and to socialist principles.

Thus spared from the capitalist imperative to generate profits, much of the wealth generated by the Chinese economy has been directly reinvested in its future growth which, in addition to the many aforementioned advantages accruing to cooperative or socialist (in contrast to competitive or capitalist) economies, has meant that unlike capitalist economies, most of which, even prior to the Great Recession struggled to maintain a 3% exponential or cumulative annual growth rate, China managed to maintain a cumulative of exponential growth rate of around 11% for many decades! As a consequence of which, again in accordance with the communist ideology of substantial distribution of wealth "to each according to their needs" as well as to those whose physical or/and intellectual labor produce it, China has, as no less an august body than the *World Bank has acknowledged*, reduced the overall poverty rate among Chinese from 88% in 1981 to less than 0.7% by 2015, even as *2 billion, or around 30% of the those in the Capitalist economies, live, as previously noted, on under $2 a day; half of whom live on under $1a day!*

While also spared in wake of the Great Recession that hit the capitalist economies in 2008, of the apparent imperative to ensure the continuing survival of capitalism, and thus to bail out the banks and other financial institutions, China, facing reduced foreign demand for its products, invested instead in infrastructure. For example, although with few exceptions—such as the Shanghai Airport to Shanghai City magnetic levitation (Maglev) train which routinely whisks travels between the two at speeds well over 430 km/hr—in the early 2000s China had few high-speed trains, and a relatively limited subway system, it now has the world's largest (22,000 miles/35,000 km) high-speed (250–350 km/hr) rail network, and the world's three longest subway systems. Similarly, notwithstanding its initially heavy, early, investment in the previously proven coal-burning power stations, China—whose government investment in, and transition to, potentially planet saving solar, wind, and hydroelectric energy production is not restricted, as it is in the US, by unremitting opposition from the taxpayer subsidized oil, gas, and coal (fossil fuel) lobby—is now the world's leader in electricity production from renewable resources, generating over twice as much from such sources as the US. Its production of solar cells, increasing 100 fold between 2005 and 2014, while it now produces well over half of world supply. And in addition to such photovoltaic energy cells, solar-powered water heaters, which heat water and radiators directly (without electrical intervention) from the sun's heat have long been extensively employed throughout China. And as with Chinese investment in transportation and energy production, so too with information infrastructure, to the point where China currently leads the world in 5G technology for example.

Nor has the wealth generated by the Chinese economy all been directly reinvested in its future growth, but, again in accord with the government's ideological commitment and concomitant concern for general social utility or wellbeing, there is increasing investment in the creation or/and maintenance of fulfilling social and cultural spaces and interactions and so on, and the provision of healthcare and education for all, which is to say in enhancing purely ***qualitative*** aspects of life, as well as in pensions, rising wages and other financial benefits. All of which tend, of course, to be positively correlated with the ***increase in the sum total of human happiness*** that is Utilitarianism's moral yardstick.[9]

In sum then, although capitalist enterprises, which if they are to survive in a genuinely competitive, transparent, and free market, must maximize the interest or/and dividends derived from investment, which is to say maximize the ***financial*** value of output divided by input, and must therefore, other things being equal, pursue profit maximization at the expense of all else—including any less than economically optimal social utility[10]—even as, by concomitantly pushing wages down and production up, this inevitably culminates in capitalism's self-destructive crises of overproduction, communism, and socialism, by way of contrast, face no such ***moral***, or indeed ***pragmatic***, not to say ***ontological*** dilemmas. Rather, relieved of

[9] See Chapter 8, footnote 1.

[10] From which we may, perhaps counterintuitively, infer, as previously implied, that any funding, by capitalism, of economically unproductive social welfare projects—such as those associated with care for the young, the aged, those among the chronically ill who will not return to productive labor, the creation or/and maintenance of fulfilling social and cultural spaces and interactions, and the like—is a direct function of its failure to maximize its efficiency; a failure which it can only survive if, insofar and so long as it does not in fact submit to competition in a transparent, *laissez-faire* or free market. Put otherwise, insofar and so long as free market competition maximizes efficiency, which is to say the value of outputs divided by the value of inputs, then this, the ***raison d'etre*** and ultimate justification of competitive free market capitalism, is, other things being equal, precisely derived, as is the interest or dividends derived from investment therein, at the expense of all else, including general social welfare! ***The search for the highest rate of return from investments, therefore, other things being equal, being, concomitantly, the search for those enterprises which contribute the least to general social welfare!***

the *competitive* capitalist imperative to generate *profit*, not only has China been able to *directly* reinvest the *quantitative* productive capacity demonstrably resulting from a *cooperative* economic system into more productively efficient (as oppose to economically profitable) clean energy, public and industrial transportation, and information infrastructure, as well as robotic production systems, pharmaceuticals, medical technology and infrastructure, semiconductors, quantum computing, artificial intelligence, and other high tech capacities, but it has also been free to, indeed ideologically obliged to, invest much of what has not been invested in such projects in more direct *qualitative* sociocultural and *quantitative* economic benefits for its citizenry. Strategies which, in addition to achieving what may be perceived as a *moral* objective, have had the undeniable *pragmatic* consequence of producing a rapidly expanding middle class, thereby boosting domestic demand; demand that not only enabled it to compensate, at least in part, for the reduction in foreign demand resulting from global capitalism's Great Recession, but, more generally, constitutes a virtuous circle which, the coronavirus notwithstanding, enables its economy to continue growing at a healthy rate, and thus to underwrite even greater commitments of the same sort.

Thus unlike the US for example, which, as already noted, has seen a decline of over 30% or more in the *inflation adjusted* median wage in the 25 years from 1982 to 2007, and a concomitant, and still ongoing, contraction of the middle class, and which, post the Great Recession and pre cardiovirus pandemic struggled to achieve a relatively anemic 2.5% cumulative growth rate, or other capitalist economies, such as those of Greece and Spain, who saw a substantial decline in their GDP even prior to the pandemic, China's cumulative or exponential growth rate which was, prior to the Great Recession, as previously noted around 11%, had not dropped lower than 6% prior to that pandemic. Thus while in the 25 years to 2007 the US economy GDP, growing at approximately 3% exponentially, as noted, increased 2 fold, the Chinese economy, growing at approximately 11% exponentially, increased about 15 fold, even at 6% exponential growth rates we might expect the Chinese economy to grow 4 fold in the time it will take that the US economy, growing at 3% exponentially, to grow 2 fold, or double; China becoming the leading world ecnomy in the process!

Clearly then, whether we define general good either in narrow, *quantitative* economic, terms, or more broadly in *qualitative* terms, as the above once again demonstrates, contra Adam Smith's claim that the pursuit, by each of us, of our individual self-interest will maximize, or even promote, the general good, on the contrary it often substantially diminishes it; a problem that is only exacerbated by wide disparities in wealth, and therefore in the concomitant disparity in individuals' opportunities to promote their own interests, often at others' expense, in the free economic marketplace.[11]

[11] Thus in addition to the argument against Smith's view that each, in pursuing their own self-interest, will maximize the sum total of human wellbeing outlined in Chapter 8, footnote 4, wide disparities in wealth will not only mean that the wealthy will be able to pursue their economic wellbeing at the expense of the poor, but the diminishing marginal utility of wealth (see Chapter 12, footnote 3 and Chapter 21, footnote 6) means that the increase in human happiness that they derive in doing so is, after a point, likely to be increasingly less than would be derived by the poor were the same capacity to direct resources available to them. Their lack of efficacy in this regard being remediable by direct government intervention in order to achieve the redirection of resources to the production of goods and services with the greatest social utility.

CHAPTER 18

# International Cooperation and the Interaction of Socialist and Capitalist Economies

**Abstract** China's "Belt and Road" international cooperation in building transportation, health, education, and trading infrastructure, which develops local expertise in furtherance of future productive trading relationships, is contrasted with the US and other capitalist economies' military support of foreign elites complicit in neo-colonializing exploitation of resources and labor to their own benefit. This, together with its "China 2025" investment in advanced energy, transportation, production, pharmaceutical, medical, communication, computing, and other high tech capacities, is enabling China to increasingly challenge many sectors of the previously technologically leading capitalist nations' economies. While its financing of the debt incurred by capitalist economies by their extension of credit to ameliorate crises of overproduction, and their (capitalist economies') concomitant corporate bailouts, has enabled China to acquire interests in much foreign real estate including ports, and many capitalist corporations and so on.

**Keywords** Belt & Road cooperation • Neo-colonial exploitation • China 2025 technological investment • Chinese port and corporate acquisitions

Turning to the future, as a consequence of its increasing technological prowess, China, admittedly *not entirely* unlike the capitalist economic



S. Glynn, *The Economic Logic of Late Capitalism and the Inevitable Triumph of Socialism*,
https://doi.org/10.1007/978-3-030-52667-2_18

neo-colonizers, has, *as part of* its $1 trillion "Belt & Road" *partnership* project involving no fewer than 120 countries, drawn in other, in many cases less technologically and economically developed countries at the base of a multinational economic structure that has enabled its economy to utilize many of their resources, as well as some of their comparatively low-cost labor.[1] A strategy that has enabled it, along with its $300 billion "China 2025" investment in solar power, robotics, electric and autonomous cars, aircraft, semiconductors, quantum computing, artificial intelligence, pharmaceuticals, aerospace and other energy, transportation, communication, production, medical, and hightech capacities, not only to move ever further up the value-added production curve, but to challenge, not infrequently overtaking, many sectors of the previously technologically leading capitalist nations' economies. For example, Chinese electric car manufacturer Nio[2] is poised to become a major competitor to Tesla and other electric car manufacturers, while General Motors agreement with the SAIC Motor Corporation of China to construct electrically powered vehicles seems to have been primarily driven, not, as one might have imagined, by GM's desire to have access to China's cheap labor, but by its desire to acquire key Chinese technical expertise in the construction of such vehicles, and SAIC's desire to have vehicles built in the US, in order to have access to US markets unfettered by tariffs on foreign auto imports! Furthermore, Huawei has plainly and publically demonstrated that it has already left the US and other competitors far behind in its provision of technology for world spanning 5G communications infrastructure. Such technological prowess, with the associated "Belt & Road" project, helping to account for China's continuingly high levels of GDP growth, and the rapid expansion of its middle class.

However, in marked contrast to both earlier forms of colonialization, and currently economic neo-colonizing *capitalist* economies such as the

[1] Indeed not only have the Chinese long been active in pursuing agreements to extract energy, rare earths and lithium and cobalt, and so on (required for manufacture of electric motors for automobiles) and many other resources from many African countries, but they have in recent years taken to outsourcing the production of textiles, clothing, shoes and other more basic, technologically "low end," goods to Vietnam and Cambodia and so on, just as the West previously outsourced low end production to China and other, hitherto less developed, economies.

[2] Nio's ES6 & 8 already outperform Tesla's equivalent on almost every metric, including range between recharges, while its high-performance EP9 holds the Nuremburg racing circuit lap record.

US, whose predominant *modus operandi*, driven by their mutual ***competitiveness***, has been to install and/or support governments that are prepared to collude with them in the *exploitation* of their nations' resources and/or population/workforce, and who is even prepared to engage in warfare to secure resources, the Chinese have adopted a very different approach. Accordingly, even while deriving relatively cheap resources and labor from those less developed than they, China, informed by the *socialist* principle of ***cooperation***, has assisted in the development of infrastructure and skills of these less developed economies, to the mutual advantage of both the Chinese and their partners' populations. Thus for the cost of a single F 35 fighter jet, the Chinese have, for example, reportedly not unusually been able to provide to those with whom they have partnered, a working port, two hospitals, five schools and about 400 kilometers of road. And in contrast to those client states economically neo-colonized by the US and others, where much of the money provided to them for resources and ostensibly for economic development, has ended up, via shell companies set up by the ruling elite, in foreign bank accounts, the Chinese oversight and supervision of infrastructural and other economic development has meant that these projects have been undertaken and completed, and that local contractors and their workforces have often been intimately involved, with or without Chinese co-workers, and have received experience, training and pay, for the work they have put into them. This then contributes both to their future value as cooperative partners and to their current demand for Chinese goods, as well as enabling them to reinvest whatever surplus they generate into their own economic and technological development. A circumstance that, so far from being predicated upon *the capitalist ideology of **competition***, is predicated upon a happy coincidence of *economic pragmatism and the communist ideology of **cooperation**, that thus constitutes a rising tide that does indeed lift all boats.*

Not that, as previously noted, China has been unprepared, when necessary, to adopt certain aspects of the behavior of capitalists as it sometimes must when working with *competitive* capitalist economies. Thus just as capitalism's *competitive* pursuit of profits has, by putting downward pressure on wages and concomitant demand, left capitalist economies such as the US with little alternative than to extend credit to its workforce in order to buoy up demand, the Chinese, whose economic participation as suppliers of labor—be it to the same US capitalists or their Chinese intermediaries, or to other and/or their own producers and competitive exporters—has, in a *competitive* global market, put downward pressure on the wages, and thus the aggregate demand of, the capitalist economies, have for the same reason extended credit to the US and other capitalist economies. The consequently continuing demand from capitalist economies, together with the free flow of resources, labor, products, and ideas playing a key role in enabling the Chinese to grow their own economy. An international extension of credit which—while it may have softened, and continues to soften, the impact on the Chinese economy of the 2008 economic meltdown of capitalist economies and ongoing decline in demand from the consumer-oriented middle classes of the capitalist economies—entailing, as does the domestic capitalist economies' extension of credit to their domestic workforces, a concomitant debt servicing obligation, is ultimately no less unsustainable. That is to say that just as the competitive market, in driving down wages eventually necessitates individual borrowing and concomitant debt obligations, interest payments on which will, other things remaining equal, further exacerbate *individuals'* problems, and ultimately render them bankrupt, so too with *nations*.

Thus just as with Greece, whose National Debt of around 175% of its GDP, meant that much of its borrowing was used to pay the interest on its debt, leaving little either to invest in potentially supply boosting technological and other economic infrastructure, or, even if the terms of such borrowing allowed it, to bolster aggregate demand, a circumstance which therefore provided no reasonable route to economic recovery, the US—with annual balance of payments deficits not unusually in the $1 trillion range, and a National Debt of approximately 106% of GDP (or an average of well over a quarter of a Million dollars per household of 4, which is to say, to many such families, the cost of a house)—is beginning to confront the same consequences.

*In short then, it is clear that the capacity to ameliorate the crisis of overproduction, inherent in the logic of free market capitalist competition, by credit or borrowing, results in debt obligations which, other things being equal, ultimately tend to overwhelm the borrower. And this, irrespective of whether the borrower be the domestic consumer extended credit by a bank or other domestic financial institution, or a government borrowing—either directly on its own behalf, or on behalf of its citizens, who it will then finance—from other nations such as China, or from international financial institutions such as The International Monetary Fund, The World Bank, or The European Central Bank.* And just as the capitalist response to this 2008 crisis included the repossession of the middle class's major assets, their houses, we should not be surprised that the Chinese are acquiring US and other capitalist nations' assets at an accelerating rate.

For example, in addition to having acquired Greece's premier port, Piraeus, Chinese companies already have major investments in more than a dozen Mediterranean and other, European, ports, from Istanbul, Genoa, and Marseilles, to Bilbao, Le Havre, and Rotterdam, and are acquiring, and looking to acquire more, US corporations. Thus the world's largest pork producer, Smithfield's foods, was acquired by Shuanghui; Motorola Mobility and IBM's personal computer division were acquired by Lenovo; Friede Goldman United was acquired by China Communication Construction Company; Cirrus Wind Energy was acquired by A-Tech Wind Power (Jiangxi) and much of the AES Corp.; Chesapeake Energy, and Oil and Gas Assets are owned by China; Starwood Hotels are owned by China's Anbang Insurance Company; Ingram Micro by Tianjin Tianhai Investment Development Co.; General Electric Appliances by Quingdao Haier Co.; Terex Corp. by Zoomlion Heavy Industry Science; and Legendary Entertainment Group and AMC Entertainment Holdings by Dalian Wanda.[3]

[3] See Michele Nash-Hoff, "Should We Allow the Chinese to Buy Any US Company They Want" in *Industry Week*, January 9, 2018.

CHAPTER 19

# Political Regulation of the Formerly "Free Market" and the Greater Efficiency and Social Utility of Technological Development Under Socialism

**Abstract** Competing with socialist economies that derive benefits from internal cooperation, capitalism's *ostensibly* anti-government intervention elites turn to government for economic rescue and political protection. And this because government—allegedly incapable of running anything efficiently—ownership and/or control of Chinese industries supposedly gives them an unfair *advantage*! Furthermore, tariffs, patent and copy-right, technological transfer restrictions, and so on, aimed at protecting profits, as *per* drug patents, *inhibit the free flow of technology and ideas potentially beneficial to all humanity.* And when all else fails, ostensibly "strategic interest," "national security" or, unbelievably, "ecological" interests, are also invoked! Incredibly hypocritical in light of the external-ization of the costs of toxic pollution, greenhouse gases, climate change, hurricanes, sea level rise, and environmental refugees, by domestic oil, coal, and gas industries; notwithstanding the astronomical cost in blood and treasure subsidizing the militaristic acquisition of oil assets.

**Keywords** Anti-government hypocrisy • Restrictive trade practices • Free flow of benefits • Externalized costs

*Facing international* ***economic*** *competition from a* ***socialist*** *economic system which derives all the economic efficiencies and other advantages accruing to such an internally* ***cooperative economy****, yet unwilling on account of the*



S. Glynn, *The Economic Logic of Late Capitalism and the Inevitable Triumph of Socialism*,
https://doi.org/10.1007/978-3-030-52667-2_19

*disproportionate short-term benefits they undeniably derive from* ***competitive capitalism*** *to avail themselves of the same advantages and efficiencies, capitalist corporations have turned to national governments not only to* ***rescue them economically*** *from capitalism's internal contradictions but also* ***to protect them politically*** *from external socialist competition.* And their supposed grounds for doing so are that Chinese, and other communist and/or socialist enterprises—which, in accordance with communist or socialist principles that the government has an obligation to help in the generation of economic benefits that will accrue to its population—are often owned and/or run and/or assisted by government, thereby giving them an unfair advantage. A reason which in light of the fact that economic neo-liberal, or ideologically committed, capitalists never tire of telling us how much more efficient private enterprise is than government run, or socialist and/or communist, economies, and that it is above all on account of *its* competitive efficiency that *laissez-faire* capitalism should be tolerated and even encouraged, and consequently that governments—even of the supposedly democratically elected variety allegedly representative of the will of the people—are part of the problem rather than of the solution, is, like the US government's aforementioned \$14 trillion[1] subsidizing and propping up of capitalist corporations, as astounding as it is hypocritical.

Such hypocritical free market rhetoric notwithstanding then, capitalists and their corporations look to their governments not only to provide them with hefty, taxpayer-funded, bailouts, subsidies and loans, and loan and other financial guarantees, but also to negotiate international trade agreements. International trade agreements which, *in the interests of protecting profits*, establish patent and copyright restrictions, technological transfer limits and other intellectual property rights, regional content requirements and exclusionary trade protections, all of which *inhibit the free flow of technology and ideas that would be of such global benefit if available to all of humanity*. International trade agreements which overwhelmingly favor those nations that have the greater power to dictate terms protective of their interests and have the wealth to engage in protracted legal proceedings in "courts" whose composition and rules they also have the power to largely structure in their interests. And when all of this fails, they fall back upon ostensibly "ecological," "strategic interest," or "national security" justifications for imposing further restrictions on the supposedly free market.

[1] See Chapter 13, footnote 4.

Beginning then with anti "dumping" regulations for instance, aimed at stopping the selling of products at below the price they cost to produce. Despite receiving billions of dollars in taxpayer *subsidies* that substantially lowered the price at which its products could be profitably sold, US agri-business was, under rules negotiated by the North American Free Trade Association (NAFTA), able to prevent Mexican government tariffs on the corn that it was consequently able to export at prices below those with which indigenous Mexican farmers were able to compete, resulting in over 2 million Mexicans being forced to leave their farms, many emigrating, or attempting to emigrate, to the US in search of work! On the other hand, George W. Bush used the claim that the competitive advantage of foreign steel producers, often resulting from technological efficiencies and low wages, was due to *hidden subsidies*, as justification for imposing tariffs which were decisive in winning him political support in the key electoral battleground States of Ohio, Pennsylvania, and West Virginia, all of which significantly helped his re-election to a second term. A lesson not lost on Donald Trump whose imposition of tariffs on steel and aluminum—despite the fact that, as Forbes magazine reports, they are actually costing far more jobs amongst industrial *users* of steel and aluminum than they are saving in the steel and aluminum industries[2]—are clearly also aimed at shoring up his support in these same electorally key States. Although in what is seen by many as an attempt to exempt imports from NATO allies as well as Japan and South Korea, while restricting Chinese competition, strategic interests, rather than subsidies, are currently the ostensible grounds for such tariffs.

Indeed abandoning many of the free-trade principles that the US espouses and actively pressured other economies to sign on to when it benefited from them—and in light of well over a third of a Trillion dollar *annual* trade deficit with China, which the US administration blithely assure us, in defiance of all logic, makes China dependent upon the US rather than vice versa—the US has entered into a trade war with China aimed at, among other things, having the Chinese agree to abandon their aforementioned "China 2025" program, which clearly ain't goanna happen. Nor has their ostensibly Libertarian free market rhetoric proved an

[2] Stuart Anderson, "Tariffs Are Costing Jobs: A Look At How Many" *Forbes*, September 24, 2018. See also, for instance Eric Boehm, "Aluminum Tariff Tradeoff: 300 Jobs for $690 Million in New Taxes," *Reason.com*, December 11, 2018, and Jesse Chase-Lubitz, "The true cost of creating jobs via Trump's steel tariffs," *Politico*, February 2, 2019.

insurmountable obstacle to the Koch brothers, and indeed other US oil and gas corporations, accepting tens of billions of dollars annually in taxpayer-funded *direct subsidies*. Subsidies which pale in comparison to the indirect subsidies they enjoy. For they have been allowed to *externalize* the *astronomical geostrategic costs, in blood and treasure, incurred in fighting wars to gain access to oil,*[3] *and of providing US government-funded foreign aid to prop up the police and military of those foreign elites consequently compliant in helping US corporations' asset striping of their countries' oil and other natural resources.* Externalized costs which additionally not only also include *environmental/health costs* such as those emanating from sulfur dioxide (acid rain), nitrogen oxides, and neuro-toxic mercury, and so on, as well, of course, as the "greenhouse gas" carbon dioxide, and methane, and consequent cost of global climate change and the resulting sea level rises, flooding, and hurricanes, but also include the many conflicts, if not started, then certainly exacerbated, by the ensuing drought in

[3] Thus, absent Iraq's possession of weapons of mass destruction, and any link to 9/11, absences which were, as per "The Downing Street Memo" of 2002, apparent to British intelligence (MI6) prior to the invasion of Iraq in 2003, it seems not unreasonable to maintain that the *necessary*, although perhaps not *sufficient*, condition of the 2003 invasion was the fact that Iraq possessed 100 billion barrels of proven oil reserves, and, it was speculated, another 200 billion unproven. A view made all the more credible by the fact that the three countries that opposed the invasion were France, Russia, and China, all of which had oil extraction contracts with Iraq, (while Washington's candidate to lead the new regime was the largely exiled "Iraqi National Congress," which had signaled its intention to critically reconsider Iraq's existing oil contracts) and by the fact that the two major protagonists were the US and the UK, both of which had extensively underutilized oil extraction capacity and technical know-how. Nor is this view rendered any less credible by the fact that the first priority of the invading army was to secure the oil fields, and extinguish fires set by a retreating Iraqi army, rather than ensuring the security of Iraq's civilian population—large numbers of whose grotesquely tortured bodies, resulting from massive inter-sectarian conflict, were turning up daily in Bagdad and other major Iraqi cities—the alleviation of whose suffering, under the ruthless dictatorship of Saddam Husain, was nevertheless touted as a major reason for the invasion. And let us not forget that the first and most significant action of Paul Bremer, "proconsul" of the occupational force, was to pass a series of orders and laws opening up Iraqi assets to foreign ownership. Nor that one of the three reasons that Osama bin Laden—who in fact, despite the US administration's claim to the contrary, proved to have no links to Iraq and Saddam Husain, whatsoever—gave for the destruction of the World Trade Towers, which housed many US investment banks and financial institutions, was that the US had stolen the resources of the Arab world. A pattern certainly discernable in the US return to Syria to protect its oil fields, following its abandonment of its Kurdish allies there (see Chapter 13, footnote 2).

the equatorial and sub-equatorial regions of the world.[4] *Conflicts, drought and flooding,* which are driving the *political and economic refugee and migrant* crisis for which the European Union and others, as well as the refugees and migrants themselves of course, are currently having to pay the price.

Furthermore, as if all this were not enough, the oil corporations also used their economic, and consequent political influence to intervene in the supposedly free market, to have the US government block China's oil company CNOOC's attempted 2005 takeover of US-based UNOCAL, again ostensibly on the basis of strategic interest. And while the Trump administration's clearly economically motivated attempt to intervene in the supposedly free market in order to restrict imports of foreign vehicles on allegedly *strategic* interest grounds was particularly ludicrous, especially in light of the fact that it was spearheaded by the *Commerce* Department, this has not stopped it from again invoking national security as grounds for attempting to persuade allies to block and abandon Huawei's 5G technology and networks.

Nor is economically motivated US government intervention in the supposedly free market, on behalf of capitalist corporations, by any means always quite so blatant. For instance, having developed anti-retroviral drugs to combat the HIV/AIDS epidemic, US pharmaceutical corporations found that their potential profits were threatened by reportedly superior Brazilian and Indian variants;[5] variants which, so *far from putting profits before lives, were inexpensive enough to benefit many who could not afford the US products.* Consequently it has only been by the imposition of patent restrictions within the US, and a much touted $5 billion US "foreign? aid" initiative, ostensibly aimed at fighting HIV/AIDS, but which, *in making the receipt of such aid strictly conditional upon the continued purchasing of US anti-retroviral,* that the investment by US drug companies has continued to pay off. Profits being further enhanced by the prohibition on aid recipients instructing their populations about, and supplying, condoms, which by reducing the chances of contracting aids, would have most certainly resulted in reducing the demand for such

[4] For a more detailed exposition of these latter consequences and externalized costs see, for instance, Naomi Klein, *This Changes Everything: Capitalism vs. The Climate* (New York: Simon & Schuster, 2014).

[5] Apparently, the original US manufactured regimen required taking a cocktail of different pills at different strategically determined times, while the foreign variants were much simpler to administer.

drugs! Nor is it coincidental that the major obstacle to concluding the negotiation of the Trans-Pacific "free-trade" Partnership (which was, of course, never implemented by the US) was the attempt by the US government negotiators to secure a 12-year patent protection of US pharmaceuticals, as compared to the 5-year period proposed by Australia, New Zealand, and several public health groups, who were clearly more concerned with bringing lifesaving medicines to poorer patients than proping up the profits of US drug corporations![6]

Moreover, far from government intervention encouraging investment in technological innovation by protecting it from potentially profit reducing competition as is often claimed, *insofar as the political class has been largely captured by the economic class, government intervention in the interests of established corporations and their technologies will just as likely militate against, and thus retard, the innovative technologies* that advocates of *laissez-faire* free market competition, and the "creative destruction" it supposedly fosters, never stop insisting, capitalism will promote. For example, returning to the consideration of energy technologies, if one enjoys, as the oil, gas and coal industries do, massive government subsidies, and a virtually unrestricted facility to externalize environmental and other costs, why invest in solar, wind, wave, and other "green" technologies,[7] which would reduce the value of your "sunken assets?"

[6] The drug companies would, of course, argue, that by reducing potential profitability such reduced patents would result in reduced investment in, and thus slow down innovation of, even more effective drugs. An argument which, so far from providing justification for increased protectionism, in the view of many is why the drug industry should be largely government owned and funded, on the grounds that by cutting out profit taking, the industry could directly reinvest almost all, if not all, the wealth it generated, in further R&D; R&D aimed at optimizing health outcomes rather than maximizing profits! While this argument may, of course, also be made in favor of a National Health Care, or socialized *medical*, as well as a socialized medical *insurance*, system; an argument which seems to be justified by the fact that although the US spends about $10,000 per capita per year, or about 2.5 times more per capita on healthcare than any other nation on earth (and, given that around 30 million remain uninsured, considerably more on those who are actually insured) it currently ranks around 34th in healthcare outcomes! Moreover, although the US government is, through Medicare and Veterans' healthcare, a major consumer of drugs, which should give it some leverage in drug price negotiations, it is precluded, by virtue of legislation passed by the best politicians that money can buy, from negotiating down drug costs in the interests of we the people, whose interests it and they are supposed to represent!

[7] "Green" technologies in general being those which are non or minimally polluting, and utilize renewable or recyclable resources, while green energy technologies are those such as solar, wind, hydroelectric, current, wave, and geothermal power (which, as clean, addition-

However, surely no one really believe that if the fossil fuel industries were to lose their (taxpayer financed) subsidies and preferential tax status, and either be forced by the Environmental Protection Agency (EPA) to clean up their act,[8] and/or to pay their aforementioned (taxpayer financed) externalized costs, as well as the (taxpayer financed) costs of propping up compliant client governments and of ***geostrategic military interventions***, which are clearly necessary to enable them to continue to access and profit from the extraction of the relevant resources—as opposed to benefiting from them as did Halliburton and others[9]—that these industries could

ally enable extensive, environment friendly, resource recycling). However, as a consequence of the capture of the political process by the economic elite, the US government's current annual subsidies to oil and gas corporations are far greater than total US investment in all alternative energy technologies combined.

[8] Such is the infiltration of government by corporations that The Environmental Protection Agency (EPA), never immune from political pressure from a Congress dominated by corporate interests, was previously headed by President Trump's appointee, Scott Pruitt, who, prior to this appointment filed no fewer than 14 challenges to the EPA's clean air and water rules. Scott Pruitt whose affiliated political action committees received campaign contributions from Peabody Energy, the Southern Power Company, and Murray Energy among others. Thus while almost 2 in 5 of the US population is currently predicted to contract cancer, between 80% and 90% of cancers being environmentally produced—[see, for instance J. Higginson, "Developments in Cancer Prevention Through Environmental Control," in *Cancer Detection and Prevention*, C. Maltoni (ed.), (Amsterdam *Excerpta Medica*, 1974) pp. 4–5 and Sir Richard Doll; Prevention of Cancer: Pointers from Epidemiology (London: Nuffield Provincial Hospital Trust), p. 106, cited in Ibid, and, more generally, Samuel Epstein, *The Politics of Cancer Revisited* (Hawkins NY: East Ridge Press, 1998)]—Scott Pruitt, clearly knowing who he was working for, busily rolled back a host of EPA regulations, and removed several scientists from EPA advisory panels. Nor has the situation improved under his successor, Andrew Wheeler, a former coal industry lobbyist. Here again then we have a classic case of the fox guarding the hen house!

[9] So complete was the domination of government by capitalist, and in particular fossil fuel, interests that having largely financed the election of George W. Bush they were able, at least in respect of the executive branch of government, to dispense with the cost of financing the campaigns of political intermediaries altogether, and to assume direct control. Thus, not only was the President, like his father, an owner of an oil company, but his Vice-President, Dick Cheney, had been the CEO of oil logistics company, Halliburton—which profited greatly from no-bid government contacts to provide logistical support for US forces in Iraq and Afghanistan—while no fewer than 8 of Bush's leading advisors and executive appointees were, or had been, either owners of, and/or leading executives and/or lawyers for, oil or gas corporations. *Nor, it should be added, can it be credibly denied that the rise of the so-called Imperial Presidency is entirely unconnected to capitalism's increasing influence upon, and indeed often near domination, of this post.*

ever be economically viable in the face of competition from alternative technologies?

None of this is, of course, to imply that government intervention need *necessarily* have such negative effects. For if, instead of aiding and abetting such protection of the interests of capitalists and their corporations at the *financial, health, social, environmental and cost to life, and so on* of the general population of the planet, governments were, in furtherance of socialism, to serve the interests of society at large, then they might protect, even subsidize investment in, and otherwise promote, technologies and technological innovation likely to serve the public good. Technological innovation which, in the case of the "Green New Deal" supported by Alexandria Ocasio-Cortez and Jeremy Corbyn for instance, would, by promoting renewable energy and other "green" technologies, *avoid the financial, health, social, environmental and costs to life of pollution and global climate change, with its associated sea-level rise, increased hurricane risk, droughts and floods, and so on, not to mention otherwise unnecessary geostrategic wars, as well as massive political and climate refugee and economic migrant displacements, and the political strife they are currently causing*. Green energy technologies which, furthermore, can readily capture and convert solar and wind power into electrical energy in a highly *decentralized* manner, and which accordingly, unlike oil, coal, and gas—which require massive investment in drilling, mining, transportation, and distribution, and in relatively centralized power plants for conversion to electricity—*have less upfront investment costs. Technologies which can therefore not only cut energy costs, but in undermining the capacity of all but those backed by huge amounts of capital to supply the market, and consequently their capacity to operate as virtual monopolies, can thus begin to undermine the inequalities in wealth which, as we have seen, threaten the long term survival of the economy.*

From all we have seen above then it is increasingly clear that Contra Adam Smith's invisible or hidden hand argument (at least as it is (mis) understood by *laissez-faire*, "free market" neo-conservatives) so far from the pursuit by each of his or her apparently immediate individual self-interest leading to the maximization of self-interest and thus to a maximizing of overall satisfaction or the good of all, under *laissez-faire capitalism, individuals' and* ***individual*** *corporations' self-interested pursuit of profit takes precedence over, and is often at the direct expense of, the good of all, or social utility. Social utility which might otherwise be derived from the investment in socially beneficial technologies, which self-interest is, as we have seen, often instrumental in actively suppressing. While absent government regulation of the financial and the real economy, capitalism will, in any event, be unable to overcome the contradictions at its heart, which will ultimately result in its destruction.*

CHAPTER 20

# The Gestalt Switch from Capitalist Competition to Socialistic Cooperation as Socially Desirable and Pragmatically Necessary

**Abstract** Socialist cooperation is as *morally preferable* as it is *pragmatically necessary*. For example, given exponential population growth, modest annual growth rates result in comparatively rapidly doubling, which, even absent a modest increases in average global living standards, significantly strains resources and pollution levels, necessitating that capitalist interests in maintaining dependence on "sunken (oil, coal, and gas) assets" give way to the social utility of renewable and non-polluting energy, and the recycling it enables. Moreover, widespread adoption of socialist cooperation would ensure compensation of the workforce at levels adequate to overcoming any impending crisis of overproduction, also eliminating the "free rider" dynamic which holds back cooperatively enhanced R&D as well as the availability of the resulting technological development to all, and educational opportunities. This would result in both a reduction in poverty and an increase in self-actualization, which, in addition to arguably reducing conflict in its own right, would reduce conspicuous consumption which would benefit the environment and reduce conflict and wars over resources.

**Keywords** Capitalist competition • Socialist cooperation • Pollution • Resource depletion • Free rider • Self-actualization



S. Glynn, *The Economic Logic of Late Capitalism and the Inevitable Triumph of Socialism*,
https://doi.org/10.1007/978-3-030-52667-2_20

Having explored and analyzed the ongoing crisis in capitalism and the elements and circumstances surrounding it, it is becoming clear that any adequate response, both to its, ultimately self-destructive, internal economic, contradictions, and to the harm it is causing to the common good, requires a *Gestalt* like switch from *individualistic competition* to *social cooperation; a switch which is not only* ***pragmatically*** *necessary—in that without such a switch capitalism, seemingly along with the planet also, is doomed to destruction—but fortuitously* ***ethically or morally*** *desirable also.*

Indeed, quite apart from the threats to our survival posed by the energy industry as it is currently constituted, even were we to switch to alternative or "green" energy, there remain other, more general, threats. For instance, increasing industrial production necessary, in face of population growth, even to maintain current per capita levels of consumption requires, *at least as things currently stand*, turning more and more of the world's scarce resources into often unrecyclable junk and sometimes irreversible, and therefore cumulative, pollution at an increasing rate. Take, for instance, the world's second largest economy, China, with around 1.4 billion people or much greater than 1/6th of the world's population, which, wary of the strains on the workforce imposed by its aging population, has recently begun changing its one child (per family) policy.[1] This will, it seems, result in an increasingly rapid rate of population growth. In which case *even if China's per capita consumption or economic standard of living were held steady, this would*, in and of itself, *result in a corresponding increase in demand for resources.* However, and furthermore, although, largely as a consequence of a fall in overseas demand resulting from the Great Recession, China, as we have noted, saw its annual economic growth rate decline, from around 11% to, prior to the coronavirus pandemic, around 6% exponentially or cumulative, this nevertheless means that if and when, post pandemic, it recovers its 6% growth rate, as one supposes it will, its economy may be expected to double every 12 years. So that if other things were to remain equal this would not only result in 2X as much pollution, but require 2X as many resources *per year* after 12 years, 4X after 24 years, 8X as much after 36 years, and 1000 X (or 100,000%) as much pollution and many resources *per year*, in a little over a century! An entirely

[1] Although not all families were restricted to one child, as ethnic minorities were exempt, and many others, particularly those working in rural agriculture for example, were often allowed to have a second child if the first was a girl, nevertheless the lifting of the restriction is expected to result in a more rapid expansion of its population.

unsustainable path, which obviously requires the extremely rapid deployment, not just of "green" energy technologies, but "green" technologies in general. For only by relying as much as possible on renewable resources, and having a substantial supply of *non-polluting* energy resources that may enable us to recycle those that are not renewable, can even a *minimal* exponential population increase or/and increase in resource consumption per capita, be sustained.

Now admittedly, given its large population, and its initially desperately low standard of living, social utility required that environmental quality be sacrificed to economic growth, to the point where China recently emerged slightly ahead of even the US, as the world's number one polluter. Yet while, with a population over 4X larger than that of the US and given that lots of its pollution is the result of producing goods for foreign export—which, as already noted helped China reduce its poverty rate from 88% in 1981 to 0.7% by 2015!—this is quite understandable, nevertheless, finally (with a current annual per capita income of around $10,000) in a position to provide basic economic support for all its population, China, as a socialist economy, is refusing to allow oil, coal, and gas interests to take precedence over social utility. Thus it more than doubled its *renewable* energy output between 2011 and 2015 for instance, and it is predicted that its *renewably* sourced electricity will equal that of the entire US electricity grid by 2030.[2] While with an abundant supply of cheap, clean, energy, the recycling of a much greater proportion of non-renewable natural resources becomes feasible.

Thus *not only* does the *sacrificing of vested individual interests to social utility, that is structurally precluded by a competitive capitalist system*, make it possible, without fear for individual survival, to pay workers sufficiently well to sustain a reasonable standard of living, and in so doing concomitantly to avoid a crisis of overproduction, thereby turning a (worker) lose/(entire economy) lose situation, into a win/win situation. But further, the same principle, when applied to technological innovation, would result in the fossil fuel industry being largely replaced with renewable non-polluting forms of energy generation. This would not only reduce global climate change, together with the, previously detailed, far reaching and drastic health, economic and political effects to which fossil fuels give rise, but it would also facilitate the extensive recycling of many otherwise diminishing

[2] Mark Hertsgaard, "Last Chance for Planet Earth," *The Nation*, p. 13, November 23/30, 2015.

resources, and the reduction of geostrategic competition, and related wars, for them. While if such cooperation were extended even more generally, it would not only overcome the "free rider" dynamic that *also* inhibits technological innovation, but it would similarly eliminate this same dynamic from educational funding, along with the unrealized and underutilized technological and human potential resulting therefrom, and in so doing accelerate the attainment of general economic prosperity and human wellbeing more generally. A reduction in the poverty and the limiting of human potential which are largely responsible for the intense competitive conflicts (including wars as well as terrorism) everywhere so evident today.

Moreover, greater concern for the social utility, and greater general access to education, and the increased possibilities for self-actualization afforded thereby taking precedence over short-term profitability, might be expected to influence what, and how much, the economy produces, as well as the nature of the process of production itself. Work that is dull and/or arduous being replaced, or at least reduced wherever replacement is not possible—even at the expense of the loss of a degree of productivity, and certainly at the expense of the production of goods of little real utility—in favor of work that is less so, and even, possibly, fulfilling. A circumstance which would predictably reduce the *excessive, and often conspicuous, consumption* by which both those in unsatisfying jobs attempt to compensate for the unfulfilling *doing* in which they are engaged by excessive consumption or *having*, and to which those whose education, instead of facilitating self-actualization, has been largely restricted to job training, often turn in their attempts to alleviate boredom and to garner the attention, affection and esteem, that a genuinely self-actualizing education might both have to some degree afforded[3] even while, in any event, rendering such appreciation by others less important. All of which would undoubtedly alleviate pressures on the natural environment, and therefore further reduce many of the tensions productive of global conflict.

[3] Thus in promoting cultural and certain other interests, and, other things being equal, a reasonably interesting personality and social skills and so on, a decent education, as Oscar Wilde so astutely observed, "teaches one to despise the money it prevents one from earning."

CHAPTER 21

# Capitalist "Freedom To," Versus Socialist "Freedom From": From Lose/Lose to Win/Win, and the Chinese Socialist Paradigm Further Explicated

**Abstract** Capitalist elites who benefit enormously, at the general taxpayer's expense, from government economic intervention while ostensibly deploring it, are then simply objecting to intervention *on behalf of the general public* that might benefit from it at their (the elite's) expense. While to the objection that although laudable in theory, socialism is unworkable in practice, one may point to capitalism's internal contradiction, and further observe that more than 1 in 4 of the population in the predominantly capitalist world live on under $2 a day, while 15 million die from malnutrition or malnutrition-related diseases every year; while overall increase in standard of living, as the Chinese reduction in poverty from 88% in 1981 to 0.7% by 2015 clearly demonstrates, is facilitated by socialistically deployed technology, the development and deployment of which is often slowed by capitalist competition, and even opposed by vested interests.

**Keywords** Capitalism versus socialism • Government economic intervention • Poverty rate reduction • Standard of living increase

To an unashamedly social, not to say socialist, vision, it will surely be objected on the one hand that government intervention in the economy constitutes an unconscionable limitation on individual freedom, and is



S. Glynn, *The Economic Logic of Late Capitalism and the Inevitable Triumph of Socialism*,
https://doi.org/10.1007/978-3-030-52667-2_21

thus inequitable in *principle*, or/and on the other hand that socialism is, in any event, unworkable in *practice*.

Turning then to the first objection, it should be clear from all we have seen that there is already extensive government intervention in the economy, in the form of TARP, QE, a massive array of bailouts, subsidies, loans, and loan and other financial guarantees and incentives, insurances, copyright and patent restrictions, intellectual property rights, regional content requirements, exclusionary trade protection agreements, ostensibly ecological yet essentially economically beneficial regulations, tariffs, anti-product "dumping" regulations, "strategic" and "national security" interest caveats, and other forms of government, and indeed international agency, intrusions. Interventions which, in capitalist economies, not uncoincidentally, tend to work to the benefit of the corporate and economic elite to whom elected representative are, as we have also seen, so often beholding for political campaign contributions and other, often more direct (e.g. "revolving door") financial benefits; interventions which the economic elite who profit from such government intrusions not only offer no objection to, but actively lobby for! Clearly then, the only substantive difference between such intervention and the form of intervention proposed here, to which they object, is that while the former is aimed at boosting the profits of the already privileged owners of capital, which is to say *those who let money work for them*, often at the expense of the working and middle classes, which is to say *those who work for money*, as well as at the expense to the environment and public health and so on, the socialist intervention proposed here is on behalf of the latter. To put it otherwise, the intrusion proposed by socialists amount to no more and no less than the proposal for democratic guidance of the economic system in pursuit of general social utility or wellbeing, while the current intrusion mainly amounts, as we have seen and extensively articulated throughout, to nothing more nor less than the subjugation of what might otherwise be economic democracy and the general social utility or wellbeing it would promote, to the interests of economic oligarchs; the general population's *freedom from* exploitation, poverty, preventable disease, ignorance, environmental degradation and endless military conflict, and so on being subjugated to these oligarch's *freedom to* maximize return on capital, no matter what the human, social and environmental costs![1]

[1] For a much fuller explication of the differences between the so-called positive and negative freedoms, see Sir Isaiah Berlin, *op. cit.* (Chapter 17, footnote 1).

As for the second objection, that socialism, even if laudable in theory, is unworkable in practice, one might reply that on the contrary it is capitalism that, no matter how justifiable in terms of Adam Smith's invisible or hidden hand *laissez-faire* it may appear in theory, is, as we have demonstrated throughout, unworkable in practice. Indeed in addition to the internal contradictions embodied in its economic logic, and in addition to the adverse environmental, social, and geostrategic impacts of capitalism, even when functioning it fails on the most basic level. Thus despite the total value of the production of goods and services *per year* worldwide being approximately $88 Trillion—or equivalent to over $11,000 per head, or $44,000 for a family of 4—2 billion of those in the predominantly capitalist world, of a total world population of around 7.8 billion, live on less than $2 per day, and half of these live on less than $1 per day, *as calculated in terms of the current buying power of a Dollar in the US, while over 15 million annually, or about one every 2 seconds, die of malnutrition or malnutrition related diseases.* In light of which alone capitalism should surely be understood, by almost any standard, as a gross moral failure. While let us not forget that the overall increase in standard of living over the years has been driven not by capitalism *per se*, but as the example of Chinese clearly demonstrates, by technological innovation. *Technological innovation* which *is*, as we have seen in detail, *precluded by the economic logic of a truly competitive free market from prioritizing social welfare over private profits, just as not only its development, but its subsequent deployment also, is, as we have also seen, often likely to be slowed rather than speeded up, by free market competition, and even opposed by vested economic interests.* An economic logic which, as argued throughout, and as the fisherperson analogy demonstrates, is in any event ultimately doomed. Contrast this then to the Chinese example—whether it be understood as socialism with Chinese characteristics, socialism with capitalist characteristics, or even capitalism with socialist characteristics—for instance.

Thus in the US for example government intervention in the economy has, in accordance with capitalist ideology and its accompanying *supply side* orthodoxy, been largely geared to promoting capital's profitability; the **2X** increase of US GDP in the 25 year period between 1982 and 2007 actually being accompanied by a fall in median wages,[2] the benefits of this doubling thereby going almost, if not entirely, exclusively to the wealthy

[2] While, although, between 1982 and 2007 US median annual wage fell, as we have seen, from $46,000 to about $34,000, due to increased labor participation rates, or more people

investor class and their asset managers.[3] The fall in median wage consequently dampening demand, the annual 3% cumulative increase in GDP over this period in face of the ongoing capitalist crisis of overproduction therefore being largely credit driven, and manifesting as a couple of boom and bust "Malthusian" cycles, before culminated, as the overextension of credit necessary to sustain it inevitably did, in The Great Recession. In China on the other hand, in accordance with socialist orthodoxy, and notwithstanding the rise of some extremely wealthy individuals, (many of whom are now being prosecuted by the Xi Jinping lead politburo for corruption, etc.) wealth has been much more widely shared—poverty rates declining, as previously noted, from 88% in 1981 to 0.7% by 2015—with the consequence that during the aforementioned 25-year period between 1982 and 2007 under discussion, the Chinese economy grew, with the notable absence of such pronounced cyclical fluctuations and concomitant instability, at an annual rate of around 11% cumulative, from $287 billion to over $4.5 trillion, or about **15X!** And although it is true that, due to the crisis of overproduction, and concomitant recession in the US, Europe, and much of the rest of the capitalist world, with the accompanying loss of export markets, China's economic growth rate, prior to the coronavirus pandemic, had fallen, in stages, to a low of 6%, nevertheless, rapidly expanding domestic demand resulting from the fact that, in accordance with socialist orthodoxy, working and middle-class Chinese have participated, much more fully than have their counterparts in capitalist economies, in benefits deriving from its economic prosperity, has meant that

per household going to work, median (as many above as below) household income remaining relatively static at around $54,000.

[3] Although with a GDP of around $14 trillion and a population of around 300 million in 2007, ***average*** individual annual income in the US was well over $46,000 per head, or well over $175,000 for a family of 4 every year, clearly much of the difference between this ***average*** and the $175,000 ***median*** (as many above as below) $54,000 family income went to the top 1%, who saw their ***annual income*** increase by approximately 230% during the 25 year period under discussion; the top 1% currently "***earning***" more than the bottom 40% of US taxpayers and ***owning*** more wealth than the bottom 90% of the US population combined. [See Borosage, R. The Great Betrayal. *The Nation*, December 3, 2012, p. 14] And as with the economy up until 2007, so too, but even more so, as previously noted, with the recovery, 93% of the first year being captured by the wealthiest 1%, with 0.1%, who have doubled their ***share*** of an expanding economy, from about 10% to 20% over the past 4 decades, capturing 37% of this recovery; a recovery from a crisis which, as we have seen, ***they precipitated***, but which, as already pointed out, was largely paid for, both directly and indirectly, by the middle class!

while the US economy grew from approximately $14 trillion to around $22 trillion, in the 13 years from 2007 to 2020, as it struggled its way out of recession, the Chinese economy grew *during that period* at an *average* cumulative rate of around 8.5%—well ahead of the US and even the most vibrant European economies—from $4.5 trillion to over $14 trillion, thereby becoming the world's second largest economy.

In contrast to the US working and middle class then, whose median annual income fell by about a third, the Chinese, who, it must be acknowledged, started from a much, much, lower, economic base, have experienced a rapid rise in standard of living, not only of the fast growing, predominantly urbanized, middle classes, and of workers previously employed in agricultural as they entered into and engaged in industrial production, but of the rural agricultural or peasant class also. Thus, most of the rural housing, much of which was built by the peasants in the 1950s and 1960s, has, in marked contrast to most of the rural dwellings in the *underdeveloped* and even *developing* capitalist world, been provided with electricity, and televisions as well as refrigerators are abundant in even the most rural settings.

Notwithstanding this lifting of the rural population out of poverty however, a large proportion of China's 700 million urban dwellers earn significantly above the rural average, which has resulted in some 150 million Chinese migrating to the mainly coastal or near coastal cities in the East over the last few years.[4] And the Chinese government has responded to this influx, and the inequalities exacerbating it, as only a planned socialist economy adequately could and would do, by instituting a "Develop the West" campaign, which, in order to ensured wide public participation in the benefits of a thriving economy, is increasingly bringing industrial and commercial development, and high speed railway networks, together with higher wages, to the predominantly rural and inland Western regions of the country. Furthermore, in pursuit of the "4 Modernizations" (agriculture, industry, science/technology, and defense) proposed by Deng Xiaoping in 1977, there has been massive government investment in public education at all levels, from rural schools, to universities, to which consequently, and in accordance with the Confucian meritocratic system, rural dwellers increasingly have access. Therefore, and in marked contrast to developing capitalist economies, where the peasants who have been replaced by agricultural mechanization, and consequently flocked to the

[4] Currently in the region of 20 million per year migrate.

cities, have been insufficiently educated to fully participate in urban economies, those Chinese who are forced off, or enabled to leave, the land by increased mechanization of agriculture[5] are often much better prepared to participate productively in the urban economies to which they are migrating. This, together with avowedly socialistic "hukou" policies aimed at restricting the *freedom to* migrating to urban environments of those who nevertheless failed to acquire such skills, helps ensure the relative *freedom from* the high crime rates, and rampant drug abuse and prostitution, not to say slum dwellings and shanty towns, so prevalent in developing capitalist countries as a consequence of the influx migration of those lacking the skills to make a decent living.

Furthermore, measures such as the extension of rural pensions, access to health care regardless of capacity to pay, a minimum living allowances, and the National Development and Reform Commission (which keeps a check, through trade associations, on price collusion and cheating with regard to basic foodstuffs such as grain, oil, meat, poultry, eggs, and milk, as well as other basic commodities) have provided a substantial social safety net, and ensured that everyone gets to eat reasonably well. Indeed, not only, as noted, was the poverty rate cut from 88% in 1981 to 0.7% by 2015, but the bottom 20% of the Chinese are better off in absolute terms both than the bottom 20% of the population in any other *developing* country, and—with the possible exception of Japan, and arguably South Korea—both of which, of course, have a far higher GDP per head—indeed any other *developed Asian* country!

Moreover, in pursuit of Deng's modernizations, the government has invested a vast, and increasing, proportion of GDP in the building of technical, industrial, and commercial infrastructure some of which—in accordance with Deng's other policy, of instituting "Socialism with Chinese Characteristics" as a way of incorporating a profit generating, entrepreneurial, element into some parts of the economy where it is felt that it might motivate production or/and efficiency—is then licensed to

[5] Indeed, in light of China's proven capacity for rapid technological innovation in industry and commerce, one may speculate that the comparatively slow pace at which agricultural and other rural production technologies are being introduced is intentional on the part of government planners. For by therefore ensuring a continuing robust demand for labor in rural areas, they are able to ameliorate the instability that would be produced by rapid mass migration to the cities in search of jobs that the industrialized sector of the economy may not yet be quite large enough to offer, and many of the rural workforce not yet sufficiently educated to fill.

individuals and groups to *operate* for profit. And while this, together with Jiang Zemin's 1993 declaration that "To get rich is glorious," which signaled an attempt to go a step further toward harnessing entrepreneurial drive by allowing, indeed even promoting, a privately financed and *owned* economic sector, may lead one to conclude that the Chinese economy, despite Deng Xiaoping characterization of it, is in fact capitalism with socialist characteristics, this, even in face of the fact that parts of the Chinese economy, and in particular those trading and otherwise interfacing with capitalist economies, have indeed, as noted, been forced to take on certain competitive characteristics, would nevertheless be a grave error. For notwithstanding the fact that some parts of the Chinese economy are, as noted, either (i) Publically Owned and Privately Operated, or indeed even (ii) Privately Owned and Operated, nevertheless, as *per* socialism, these sectors are subject to extensive government regulation and, in accordance with socialist principles, to progressive taxation which is used to promote projects in the public interest. While in addition to this direct regulation and taxation the Chinese government maintain extensive indirect control over the private sector—as once *did* the then Nationalized Bank of England over the British Economy for example—via an extensively Regulated Financial System, the Lending Priorities which therefore directly reflect government policies. And even more significantly much of the Chinese economy, particularly that which produces more fundamental, if not essential, products, is comprised of either (iii) Collectively, or/ and Town or City, Owned and Operated enterprises. While most significantly—mirroring British Socialism's public or government ownership and operation of key industries until as late as the 1980s, when privatization by the Conservative Thatcher government sacrificed much of the general social welfare derived therefrom to Capitalist profiteering—much of the Chinese economy is (iv) Government or State Owned and Operated. This sector then includes core Energy Generating industries, such as coal (British equivalent, National Coal Board) gas (British Gas) oil (British Petroleum) and nuclear (British Nuclear Fuels) powered Generation, and Distribution (Central Electricity Generating Board) Iron and Steel Production (British Steel Corporation) key Transportation such as rail (British Rail) major road haulage (National Freight Corporation) aviation (British European Airways and British Overseas Airways Corporation) and Vehicle Production (British Leyland and British Shipbuilders Corporation, etc.), as well as Space Exploration (British Aerospace), not to mention Telecommunications (British Telecom) major Media Production and

Broadcasting Outlets (British Broadcasting Corporation) and Education (Oxford, Cambridge and London Universities, etc.) as well as Armaments. *Sectors of the economy which, notwithstanding their predominantly prioritizing social utility over profits, are nevertheless currently responsible for about half of China's GDP.*

In sum then the choice appears obvious to all but those who benefit, albeit, for the reasons outlined, inevitably temporarily, from exploitation of others and the environment. On the one hand *initially zero-sum, and ultimately lose/lose capitalist competition, which, requiring as it does, as a precondition of survival*, maximum efficiency or productivity, even at the expense of environmental, social and human welfare, drives down wages and other social benefits as it drives up production, thereby inevitably precipitating what, other things being equal, will be increasingly frequent and severe crises of overproduction. Crises ameliorable in the short term by credit driven, and, upon inevitable economic meltdown, taxpayer-funded, government bailouts, which is to say a perverted or negative socialism, which takes from the poor to give to the rich. Intervention which, if consumer/taxpayer demand is nevertheless to be maintained as, in order to escape such crises it must be, must ultimately entail an increasing unsustainable and foreign financed National Debt, which will therefore inevitably lead to total economic collapse, and the civil unrest, or worse, accompanying it. On the other hand, by way of contrast *win/win socialist cooperation*, which *in attempting to ensure that the economy serves the general public, rather than the other way round*, and thus prioritizing human, social, and environmental wellbeing over private profits, therefore —in line with the principle of diminishing marginal utility[6]—spreads the

[6] As this principle notes, there comes a point where the increase in human happiness—which we have argued tends to be positively correlated to the increase in economic wellbeing—to an individual or group for every additional unit of inputs of a resource, or the money that they are able to command—their "bang for the buck"—begins to diminish. Thus, for example, the increase in both economic utility and human happiness that an otherwise starving individual might expect to derive from, say, an extra $5 a day, is, other things being equal, generally much greater than that which a Millionaire might expect to derive from the same $5. A fact which therefore tends, at least on humanitarian as opposed to capitalist, grounds, to encourage spreading the benefits derived from an economy more widely and equally than, typically, does capitalist competition.

benefits deriving from the economy widely. *A strategy, which, in maintaining robust demand, avoids the economic and environmental, not to mention social and human, catastrophe, portended by capitalist competition, not despite, but indeed because, of its promoting human, and indeed social, well-being. Not of course that the progression of history will necessarily be directed by choice, for, given the essential nature of capitalism, as we can perhaps now see, its ultimate demise, brought about by increasingly persistent crises of over-production, is as logically inevitable as it is morally desirable.*

# Index[1]



[1] Note: Page numbers followed by 'n' refer to notes.



S. Glynn, *The Economic Logic of Late Capitalism and the Inevitable Triumph of Socialism*,
https://doi.org/10.1007/978-3-030-52667-2

The manufacturer's authorised representative in the EU is Springer Nature Customer Service Centre GmbH, Europaplatz 3, 69115 Heidelberg, Germany. If you have any concerns regarding our products, please contact ProductSafety@springernature.com

Printed and bound by CPI Group (UK) Ltd, Croydon, CR0 4YY
30/09/2026
02225666-0011